Perils To Pearls

Pauline Brash

Xulon
PRESS

TABLE OF CONTENTS

FOREWORD

The pearls have come in. This time, they are Pauline's Pearls.

So often, life's situations throw us sand – coarse, stinging, gritty, irritating and unstable sand. Pauline was not exempt. However, with God's help and the support of family and friends, she continued living despite the sand. Yes, she continued "pearling" night and day. Now, the pearls are in.

Pearls are formed through pain and perseverance. Pearls tell the story of one person's journey through the sometimes rough and difficult terrain of life – a journey that is lived by many innocent, vulnerable children whose future, in part, is in the hands of parents and other adults. I say in part because there is always the ever present powerful hands of God that work to produce miraculous results.

Pauline's pearls tell a great story. I have known her for over thirty years. She sparkled in the waters of affliction. She sang with a passion which was driven by the intimacy that she shared with God who imparted gifts and talents to her.

It's time for me to release you so that you can take the journey through Pauline's pearl-making process.

Read this book and laugh! Read it and weep! Read it and be encouraged! Read it and be enriched!

- W. Sammy Stewart

INTRODUCTION

TURNING POINT

The year 1996 was a turning point in my life. I was ushered into making some drastic life changing choices. These choices affected not just me, but my entire family. As the unforeseen and unexpected challenges started rolling in, I remembered a conversation which took place between a former co-worker and I. He urged me to see the parallel between myself and the character in the old movie "The Perils of Pauline."

I did not realize it in 1995, but a catalyst was about to enter my life and I would be required to choose to "fight" or "flee." So in 1996 The Tolosa-Hunt, the rare disorder became that catalyst.

I felt like I was drowning in deep, dark murky, unfriendly waters, until I reached up and He reached down to my level – I had found the "Pearl of Great Price" or better yet – He found me!

It was then that I felt the unction in my spirit to turn my PERILS over to the only ONE who was and is able to turn them into PEARLS – rare, fine, admirable and valuable jewels.

This is my story and I invite you to embark on this journey with me.

****

DEDICATIONS AND ACKNOWLEDGEMENT

~Grandfather (MR. UNDERSTAND)~

A wise old Sage, you lived to be 90 years old. You never seemed out of control and I enjoyed being in your company and having various conversations about life and Astronomy (your favorite subject). I was amazed at your vast knowledge of Creation and admired your skill and patience with your grape harbors even when the crop was not all that you expected. Grandfather, you rocked your world with four words, "UNDERSTAND YOURSELF, RIGHT AWAY!" I grew up hearing you say those words to young and old, rich and poor alike, but I never fully grasped the full essence until I became an adult and discovered the foundational scripture, Proverbs 4:7 (KJV) – "Wisdom is the principal thing; therefore get wisdom: and with all thy getting get understanding." Thank you Grandfather- we cherish your memory.

~Granny~

Granny, you gave your life unselfishly to serve not only your children but also your children's children and their children as well. You were a prayer warrior who knew the worth of prayer. In fact, you are the reason prayer burns with fervent heat in and through me to this day. You were a passionate woman of faith in Christ and you expressed your emotions unashamedly. When the Spirit moved, you would take to the streets and begin to preach, warning those who would listen. You would tell them to repent of their sins and turn their lives over to Christ. For someone who could not read or write, Granny, you impacted your world by getting the message across. You were the best cook I have ever known. Living in a third world country, you had so little to work with, yet, you were able to create many delectable meals to the delight of the entire family. Granny, you were absolutely smashing when you got dressed for church. I called you my "pretty blue eyed girl" not realizing your familial history. You had the prettiest eyes and you saw much deeper than we knew.

My prayer is that many of your virtues will be evident in our family, beginning with me and continuing in the generation of women to come. God bless you Granny and thank you for giving to the Lord. I look forward to seeing you in heaven some day, I love you!

~Aunty Inez~

I have precious memories of you, Aunty Inez. The earliest of which, is when you'd place me between your knees and comb my hair until there were nice, long and pretty plaits, as we call them in Jamaica. I was very impressed with the way you dressed, especially when you wore your Jamaica Omnibus Company's conductress uniform, you looked so prestigious! You gave me the opportunity to develop independence when traveling on public transportation. You also gave me the courage to go and pay your bills at Court's Furniture Company. Your admiration of my ability to conduct intelligent conversations in any place of business, filled me with pride. I remember your kindness most of all and I miss you very much. Aunty, you went away too soon!

~Mama~

Mama, you were like deep waters with so many secrets yet to be revealed. You had a challenging life filled with many ups and downs. I wish we had a better line of communication. We were never as close as a mother and daughter relationship should be. There were too many variables. I wish you told us about the cancer sooner, since by the time we found out the truth, it was too late. Every now and then I reflect on the teardrop as it ran down your cheek. You were like a child reaching out for an answer which seemed to evade you. I remember you transitioning and wanted to bring you back but you were ready to go and we had to let you...

~Hope~

How could it happen- was it your destiny? A mere 40 years? It still doesn't make sense to most of us. My baby sister – gone! You gave your life to serving others. What a vision you had. You were so brilliant and it scared a lot of people who did not understand. Your greatness came forth like rushing water in a waterfall. You endeavored above all, to see others become as passionate as you in pursuing their dreams, goals and visions. You left a legacy behind and your dreams are being perpetuated.

~Steve~

Twenty-seven years was all you got. You hadn't even started living yet. It just seems so unfair that you were taken out like that. The entire family misses you so much and wonderful memories live on!

~Aunty Sita~

Your early years were not as favorable to you as you would have desired. Kingsley, your only son was swept away from you at such an early age. You really did not get to enjoy him for as long as you would have hoped. I heard that he was my "little baby sitter" being three years older. He called me "Baby P" – wish I could have known him. Yet, you lived to be a full 80 years. You slept away and now you are resting in the arms of your Maker!

Chapter 1

Sing Pauline!

****Because thou hast been my help, therefore in the
shadow of thy wings will I rejoice****
Psalm 63:7 (KJV)

"Sing, Pauline!" Those words, spoken to me from childhood, signified a commission.

In 1975 I was invited to minister at a conference being held in Fort Worth, Texas. This event changed the course of my life. The invitation came from Rev. Nathaniel A. Urshan, the pastor of Calvary Tabernacle in Indianapolis, Indiana and later the general superintendent of the United Pentecostal Church International. Pastor Urshan was also a type of scout for the organization. He traveled internationally to identify and recruit talented individuals to participate in these conferences.

During Pastor Urshan's visit to our church, the Music Director, W.S. Stewart asked me to sing in the service. The anointing of the Lord came down and many were blessed. I sang "If God is Dead, Then Who's This Living in My Soul?" also "Do You Know My Jesus?" As we left the campus, I heard a voice behind me, "Pauline Chenn, we would love to have you come and sing for us at Calvary."

This invitation also taught me firsthand how faith giving really works. Prior to Rev. Urshan's visit, I received an unexpected blessing in the form of a check for $40. I felt impressed to give it back to the Lord sacrificially. I had no idea where the return would come from. I have vivid memories of my Pastor, Bishop Paul Reynolds requesting my presence in the church office and presenting me with the letter from "overseas." The letter contained a check for $400. Pastor Urshan sent the money to pay for my flight to the conference. This was a 10 fold increase on what I had given. It was a miracle and it proved to me that no one can outgive God!

This opportunity was such an honor for me and I was determined to make the most of it. My first priority was to devote my time to fasting and prayer and then to preparing for the trip. This was an intense time for all of us. Although I would be leaving my children Andrew, Charmaine and Michelle for three weeks, they still shared in the joy of it all. I made plans for them to stay with their favorite aunt Beverly and that was more like a vacation for them. God supernaturally provided everything I needed for my trip. My sister offered to style my hair and gave me the most appropriate "Pentecostal hairdo" she was capable of.

My pastor's wife Beth Reynolds and another friend Wilma Hamilton gave me more than enough beautiful dresses for the trip. I was ready for this new season in my life.

The day finally came and I was filled with nervous excitement. As I look back, I realize how overdressed I was for my trip, but no one said a word. I had been a member of this church and organization for only three years and I learned early on that one's appearance was quite significant. Needless to say I tried very hard to adhere to the standards and dress codes, with many comical experiences, like this one, along the way.

I made it to the conference and after the main service, they announced the names of all those who would
be ministering in the Songfest. There must have been a
trillion butterflies in my stomach. My legs felt wobbly. I
had visions of not being able to move and tripping over
my own two feet. I was sitting beside Pastor Urshan's
wife and all I could manage to say was "I'm so nervous."
She smiled at me and told me that everything would be
all right. I began to muster up whatever faith I thought
I had. I even tried praying but could not find any words.
Then I heard my name. I was being presented to the
Conference.

How I wished that mama was there. She was the
first to recognize my gift and love for singing. When I
was little she would have me stand on a chair, so that
people could see me perform my songs or recite poems.
I would have loved for her to see me stand in front of
25,000 people singing with everything I had. All those
years of training were paying off. As I walked towards
the podium, I quickly scanned the crowd searching for
a familiar face. Panic rose up in me as I remembered
that I had not rehearsed with these band members! The
musicians from Jamaica were so nervous that the conference musicians had to accompany me on the song.

I opened my mouth and belted out, "IF GOD IS
DEAD, THEN WHO'S THIS LIVING IN MY SOUL?" The
musicians played, the people worshipped and I sang. I
was not shaking anymore because of fear or nervous-
ness, but now under the Anointing of the Holy Spirit.
The Lord had come through for me one more time! After
the Conference I was taken to Indianapolis, Indiana to
record for a segment of the "Harvestime" radio program.
I was so proud when they aired it in Jamaica. This was
quite a monumental occasion in my life and I am forever
grateful.

While in Indianapolis I was also invited to sing on
one of the college campuses. It was quite a different

experience from life in Jamaica and I was a little nervous, but I made it through. My prayer was always that someone would come to know Christ as a result of the ministry. As a special treat, my airfare was also paid to go to Brooklyn, New York to spend another eight days with my mother and siblings. Then back to Jamaica. I was experiencing the flavor of God's uncommon favor!

It was all reminiscent of a decision I made four years earlier. In 1971, I entered a local Talent Hunt sponsored by the Jamaica Broadcasting Corporation. At my audition, I sang acapella and they entered me into the competition. I chose a song which Stevie Wonder recorded entitled, "Abraham, John and Martin." The miracle was, I had only one day to learn it and I won first place. The song told the story of how the lives of these three men affected the world. It was the right song for me. This experience exposed me to a little of the show business and entertainment arena.

It swept me up like a whirlwind. Everywhere I went there was someone calling out my name. They had seen the "Talent Hunt" show on television and the sitcom, "Sweet and Lovely." My face became known. The local newspapers included me on their entertainment pages. I was also awarded a contract to sing at the Playboy Nightclub in Ocho Rios.

I believe the Lord used my boss, to say "no" for me. I remember how he put his hand on my shoulder and he spoke these words, "Chenn, it's either Playboy or this job, you can't have both". I know that the Lord helped me to make the right decision. When I thought about my three children I chose to stay. I could not leave them to go chasing after clouds.

Various recording studios were making special offers for me to sign contracts and record with them. I decided to go with Dynamic Sounds, which was a well known recording studio in Jamaica at the time. They planned on me recording the song, "Where You Lead," which was written by Carol King. My producer was quite sure we had a "hit" on our hands. All we needed was Byron Lee and the Dragonaires to return to Jamaica, lay more music on the track and the project would've been complete. The band was delayed and in that short span of time my emancipation from a lifestyle of sin occurred. In fact, two weeks after I recorded the song, I received the Holy Spirit.

My newfound fame was short-lived since the Lord had other plans for me. I did not know it then, but the Scripture Jeremiah 29:11 was meant for me, "For I know the plans I have for you, declares the Lord, plans to prosper you and not to harm you, plans to give you hope and a future."

Chapter 2

Highlights From My Childhood

*** *For thou hast possessed my reins: thou hast covered me in my mother's womb. I praise thee because I am fearfully and wonderfully made...* ***
Psalm 139:13 – 14a (KJV)

I was born in Yallahs, St. Thomas. This area got its name from Captain Yallahs in 1671. Then in 1828 it became the birthplace of the first Baptist church in Jamaica, W.I. I was born in a house just below the hill where my maternal grandfather resided. As a child I would always look forward to seeing the house when I visited my god-mother (Goddy Vic). On subsequent visits, there was only a "stump" left as a reminder that a house was once there. On my last visit to Yallahs in 2000 Goddy Vic had passed away two weeks before I arrived. The "stump" was removed and a new house was in its place.

My earliest recollections began in Bath, St. Thomas. I have vague memories of my life from as young as two years old. One of which was when I acquired the nickname 'Pepper'. Someone placed a bowl of hot peppers on a table that was within my reach. I ended up eating a good portion of those peppers and the only thing that could ease the pain was the coconut oil they gave me to drink. After that experience, the name just stuck.

My memories of Nursery School range from being fed cookies and milk made from 'milk powder' to sleeping on a cot for my afternoon nap.

Another memory is of the Anglican and Baptist church in Bath. I always wondered why they had the cemetery in front of the Baptist church building and why it was so close to where my nursery class was held.

The botanical gardens in Bath bring back pleasant memories. It was only the second of its kind, to be developed in the western hemisphere. I still remember 'outings' in the garden; the smell of moist dirt, fragrances emanating from the special flowers and plants like Spathodea, Poinciana, Jacaranda and Cinnamon. The garden also had fruit trees like Navel Orange, Tangerine, Bombay Mango, Jackfruit and most importantly Breadfruit. Another interesting plant grown there is Strychnos, which is used to make medicines; ironically it's also used to make the deadly poison, Strychnine. There was something magical and mysterious about this garden. It seemed like a maze to me and it amazed and intrigued me. The garden was so vast and I was always curious about what I might find in the next row. I felt safe there and was often reluctant to go back to my normal life.

At age five or six, there was a small cloud of darkness that would pop its ugly head in the midst of all the brightness and beauty that surrounded me. It was *"those dirty old men."* The shoemakers across the creek and the seemingly harmless grandfather of the family my parents rented a house from. Thoughts of those old creepy fingers touching me, run across my mind causing me to cringe. I wonder how they seemingly got away with violating me. Where were the concerned citizens of the day who would expose and speak out against such abuses? Unfortunately, they did not seem to exist in those days.

Mothers, grandmothers, aunts and uncles would look the other way when a little girl was violated by an "elder" in the community. It was so "hush hush" one did not dare open their mouths to speak out against the injustices for fear of being ostracized. They are all dead and gone now, and waiting for the judgment of all the deeds they did on earth. I am alive and am able to testify as an overcomer! I wish they were alive to be held accountable and brought to justice!

Early in life I was very insecure and when I acted this out I was often misunderstood. As the oldest of ten children on my mother's side, I was always under scrutiny. It seemed like I was constantly corrected for something they felt I had done wrong. The only time that I felt sure of myself was when I was singing. For that, I must thank my mother who was the first to recognize my artistic abilities. When I participated in the Easter and Christmas programs at the Baptist church, she would make sure I wore the prettiest dresses and accessories. She also supported my activities in the school events at Festival.

You could say that my mother in her own way became my singing mentor. She played a major role in shaping me to be a young performer. Mama's mentor was her very strict godmother but she received a love of singing from my grandmother. I can recall hearing her sing. She had a strong, vibrant second soprano and when she sang her voice resonated through the house. It commanded much respect and reverence to the One she was singing about. Mama recognized my talent and encouraged me to sing, recite poems and to be involved in church and school drama. During this time, we lived in White Horses. This district received its name from the white foamy waves of the Caribbean Sea; which appeared to be prancing and dancing like Lipizzaner horses before coming to land on its shores.

Education – Mama's style:

I also credit my passion for reading to my mother. Thankfully, she imparted to me what she received from her godmother. Mama would tutor me after school. She drilled me on time tables and the names of Columbus's three ships-the Pinta, Nina and Santa Maria. I will never forget the big rock in the back yard where I would be positioned for what seemed like endless ages. Most often, I was not allowed to leave that rock until I had met her requirements.

If I failed the test and it got dark she had to bring us in whether to eat dinner or otherwise, but I knew a punishment was coming. For me, the worst punishment was being locked out of the house while it was pitch black outside. All I could see in front of me was the "out house" and the forest. In the daytime, the trees in the forest appeared friendly but at night, when nothing was really visible to the eye, those same trees became my enemies. The scary cries of the owls ringing out in thunderous tones, terrified me even more. I battled for many years with a fear of the dark.

As soon as I could read, I became the designated messenger. It was my job to deliver 'stuff' to my aunt Inez who lived in Bath. My mother would get me all dressed up in my prettiest dress and pink cockle shell accessories. My mode of transportation was the milk truck. So around five o'clock in the morning, I would be up and dressed, a little sleepy but excited since I was going to be traveling for quite a while sitting beside Edgar the milk truck driver.

I was disappointed and humiliated when Edgar would stop in Morant Bay to pick up his girlfriend. Imagine my horror when I realized that she would not only have to sit in the front of the truck with us but she would be positioned right in the middle between Edgar and me. I couldn't wait to reach my destination. The best part is that the sting from the incident only lasted a moment and was soon forgotten during the visit with my fascinating Aunty Inez. She would also visit us during our school breaks, and this gave my siblings and I the chance to play outside. We did not have the luxury of owning or playing with toys from a store, except a doll now and then. But, we loved making up games and one of my favorites was called "moonshine baby." I must add that this game had nothing to do with the infamous illegal liquor that used to be made in America.

Chores

No matter how hard I tried, I could not hold a bucket of water on my head. It was the custom for those living in that part of the country to collect water from the 'stand pipe' in little buckets and fill a 'drum pan.' This water would be used for cooking, bathing and even drinking and was expected to last for awhile. I believe my mother would boil our drinking water, thank God for that!

I would watch the other children make the cotta, which was a towel used to create stability for the buckets to rest on their heads. It required correct positioning on the head so the neck could maintain balance. I was not able to achieve this great feat and after a few futile tries, I was excused from that chore. To my delight, I was still qualified to go with Mama and the other women on Monday Wash Day at the river. These were fun times just splashing in the cool water with the other children from the village. It was as though I did not have a care in the world. While the women chatted among themselves, the children swam or pretended to swim; dunking each other and squealing at the top of their lungs out of sheer joy.

I was not a total failure at doing chores because one of my areas of success was in washing dishes at the outdoor fireside. Every morning before school, I could be found there with ashes and cucumber or 'susumber' leaf as my dishwashing detergents. I always spent that time singing. There were two wise men, Baab and Mr. Alexander who rode by on their way to the farm but they would stop for a short moment to greet me and listen to me sing. Baab called me "Cookie" and told me that he hoped I would become a matron in the hospital some day. He said "may the ants come to let me know that you made it!" In the evening on their way home they would come bearing gifts – honeycomb and sweet ripe bananas. I loved chewing and sucking the comb until there was no honey left. I knew it was empty when I found myself chewing on wax.

Pink shorts era

During one of Mama's pregnancies with another of my siblings, I was sent to the shop down the hill, to buy her saltine crackers and orange soda. So off I went in my little pink shorts, my blouse and slippers. I would also buy 'shag' tobacco for Papa. I did not like to handle 'shag' since the scent was so overwhelming and made me nauseous. Of course, children were not allowed to complain so we just did what we were told. I met some friends at the shop and began to talk and just 'hang out.' Time flew by and before long it was dusk and I realized that I had overstayed my time. I hurried home and just as I reached the path to the house, there was Papa sliding down the trunk of the Ackee tree which was at the gate. I did not pause to have a conversation with him; instead I took off running with the crackers, orange soda and shag in hand. Papa started to run after me shouting my name. Behind me I was also gathering onlookers who decided to join in the chase. Finally, someone caught me and turned me over to him.

I later found out that Papa wasn't chasing me because I was in trouble. He climbed the tree to get Ackee (this is the national fruit of Jamaica, and is cooked with salt fish to create the national dish) for dinner and saw a fierce chameleon lizard that could change colors from green to black. It was said that whenever it changed, it was getting ready to strike. Papa knew this and was 'sliding' down the tree, to save his life. When I retell this story to my children and grandchildren, it stirs up much laughter.

It seemed like every time I wore my pink shorts I got into trouble. I remember being fascinated with the post mistress who would travel by horseback to and from the post office. Whenever I got a chance to see her I was mesmerized and hoped that someday I could be like her. I tried very hard to be on my best behavior when I was in the vicinity of the post office. But one day, I failed miserably. A girl came to the shop where my Aunty worked and hit my brother in his back. I loved my brother and felt that as his older sister, I needed to protect him. Well, I moved into action and before you could say "pink shorts" I was in a fight and we were rolling down the hill. Inside I was thinking Mrs. Hercott is looking at me and shaking her head in disbelief. There went my honor.

Simple childlike Faith:

Mama seemed to have a baby every year. Some lived a short while and then went back to God. She gave birth to ten but only six survived. Steve came when I was approximately seven years old. From his birth, I was very close to him. In his early years he was a "sickly" child. I recall him having pneumonia and we did not know if he would make it. I remember being sent to shop for groceries. While I was there, I made an executive decision to buy a red balloon for Steve. When I got home, I gave it to him and he laughed! He was healed at that very moment! (Proverbs 17:22)

Up until nine years of age, the only family I knew was Papa, Mama, Granny, Aunty Inez and my maternal siblings. Papa was a strong farmer, with his donkeys and setting the coal kilns. He also grew the most wonderful tomatoes, bananas, yams and gungo peas. On one occasion, at the request of Papa, my brother Carl and I rode the donkey to the field. The donkey bumped his hoof into a stump in the road and fell.

Although we survived to tell the story, after we fell off the donkey, we vowed to never attempt that again.

On one fateful day, I was introduced to my biological father. I later learned that he was what some would call a "rolling stone", with multiple women and children in his life. I was curious as any child would be, to find out more about my father and my other siblings. He wanted to get custody of me and to change my last name to his. He offered to bring me to Kingston with him and my mother let him take me. Maybe she was reaching out to him to claim me or to rescue me. I imagine that she felt I would have a better quality of life with him. She never asked me how I felt about her decision. I was just expected to cooperate and I did.

Where he brought me, was a very tense and unhealthy atmosphere. I experienced moments of utter despair as I felt trapped and wondered if there was a way out. My freedom was taken from me. I was even forced to attend a school that was way too advanced for a nine year old. This was a world unfamiliar to me and I could not connect. But God heard my cry, and sent Granny to my rescue. I pleaded with her to take me home. She did the best she could to shorten my time in that evil place and soon I was transitioned to stay with my Uncle until Granny got a place of her own. I was registered in Rousseau Primary School where I was now in class with children my own age and doing school work that was right for me. Finally, a reprieve!

Here at Rousseau I was a member of the "Pauline club" – to qualify, you had to have long hair that could be tied with a bow. There were about four of us and we even had body-guards! Plantain tarts were my favorite thing to buy for lunch at a little shop on the hill near the school. Granny would pack my lunch box with healthy food but I would substitute that lunch for plantain tarts or sweet potato pudding. I paid dearly for those decisions by becoming quite ill with gastroenteritis.

Mama came from the country and took me back to White Horses. After a few visits to the Morant Bay hospital, I was registered in the White Horses Primary School where I excelled in Reading. As a result, I was skipped to the highest level in class and nominated as afternoon Reading Class leader. One of my class mates who was also from my neighborhood, did not appreciate my correction in one of our sessions and challenged me to an after school confrontation. I took the challenge and soon found out that I had some "body-guards" here as well, even though there wasn't a "Pauline club" at this school. They were instrumental in ending the conflict.

Back to Kingston and Tarrant Senior School

After some years had passed, I was transitioned back to Kingston to attend Tarrant Senior School. My friend Maria and I influenced and challenged each other into doing some daring things. She challenged me to enter the school beauty pageant. The initial pageant requirement was a bathing suit competition where the contestants had to model in front of the judges to find out if they were chosen or disqualified. I did not own a bathing suit but I would not be denied. I promptly asked my aunt Hyacinth more fondly known as Auntie Sita, if she would lend me her bathing suit. She did, without hesitation and into the tryouts I went. I was about 12 years old.

My aunt was a medium sized woman and around 5 feet 5 inches tall. I was small and short. I put her bathing suit on and it literally just 'hung' on my small frame. It must have been a sight to behold, but Maria still nudged me on. I don't really recall how I made it through the ordeal. Needless to say, I was not chosen to enter the pageant and did not walk away from the competition with a trophy. If they had a singing competition, I may have stood a better chance at winning. Life settled back to normalcy and soon I forgot all about that comical event. Children are so resilient.

Chapter 3

The Story Behind The Glory!

***Now thanks be to God,*
*which always causeth us to triumph through Christ...****
II Corinthians 2:14 (King James Version)

Seeking Identity – THE JOURNEY

My stepfather inherited a house and property through the death of his brother. We were now living on Olympic Way in Kingston. The entire family was now reunited, including Aunty Inez and Granny. I felt bombarded by the chaos and confusion I experienced there. My maternal siblings seemed to be floundering in a sea of hopelessness and I just wanted to escape.

Before long another transition took place in my life, as my biological father showed up again. His presence always seemed to put my life into a whirlwind. I never felt secure and questioned his motives for wanting to change my name. Mama refused a second time and this just further complicated the matter of my identity.

My love for reading, led me to the Tom Redcam Library after school one day. It was there that I would have an encounter for which I was not prepared. I remember so clearly, when the clerk asked for my name, I said "Pauline Campbell." Immediately, I heard a girl say, "Oh no, that's not your name. You are my sister!" I turned around in the direction of the voice and could not believe what I experienced. Blood was reaching out to blood-our father's blood!

I felt a connection and knew instantly that these were my siblings – a sister and a brother. I went home to share the good news with Mama. My sister Beverly also shared the news with her mother. Both of our mothers were not happy. On the other hand, once Daddy found out about our chance encounter, he returned to claim me.

I had such mixed emotions. I wanted to go with Daddy, yet, I felt an obligation to stay with Mama especially since she was pregnant again. In my desperation, I made the choice to leave and before long I was taken to Lawrence Tavern where Daddy resided with my Stepmother and paternal siblings.

It was an eye-opening experience for me. A stark contrast to the life I lived back in Kingston. There was a strong emphasis on education and my siblings here appeared to be striving for a better life. I felt challenged to do the same but at times could hardly keep up the pace considering my previous environment. I was still trying to find my identity and needed a "voice" in order to survive. This new family dynamic was still not what I was looking for. It was so different and before long I found myself swept up in an overwhelming emotional tsunami.

I was experiencing sensory overload. And it was evident that my connection to this other side of my family was not without its challenges. Regardless of my desire to fit in, I still felt like an outsider. It was during this time that my insecurities resurfaced as I was subjected to negative and sometimes detrimental situations. Meanwhile, the rejection I felt as a girl followed me into young adulthood and seemed to guide me into unhealthy relationships.

There are no words to express how devastating one vile act is, to a young woman's self esteem and self worth. The effect is even more damaging when her aggressor is not held accountable. Everyday women are faced with the burden of carrying guilt and shame after being victimized. It's no wonder Jesus came to the rescue of Mary Magdalene. None of the men she had sexual relations with, were brought into accountability. Instead they joined the mob of accusers who were ready to stone her. Jesus knew their hearts and challenged them while covering her and releasing her from all of that – He said in St. John, chapter 8 "Neither do I condemn thee, go and sin no more."

I lived in denial for many years and found it quite difficult to be honest about the hurts and pain that I had experienced. I was a victim but I am now a survivor of incest and sexual abuse. It is by the grace of God that I'm able to share my story and boldly proclaim that God's love is powerful enough to turn scars into stars, trials into triumphs and pain into praise! I am not just a survivor, I AM AN OVERCOMER!

Pearls of Promise:

The dark days are over and generational cycles have been and are being broken. This is a New Day and Love and Forgiveness win-hands down!

Chapter 4

Challenges and Changes

***He sent from above, He took me,
He drew me out of many waters***
II Samuel 22:17 (King James Version)

I became a wife, mother of three children, and eventually a Christian between the ages of 17 and 22. Unfortunately, my conversion produced much conflict in my marriage. My husband began to act more like an enemy than a loving spouse. As God transformed my life, the contempt he had towards my conversion made him increasingly dangerous to me. I remember when he made a vow to kill me. On several occasions I was forced to go into hiding because of his threats. I remember the terror I felt when he would show up at my job or at the church and demand to see me. This is when my friends put love into action. They were totally committed to protecting me and my children. I'm so grateful for the times they positioned themselves at strategic points to be "look outs" when he was on the rampage. When I was told that he carried a gun, I knew that given the chance, he would use it. The leaders in my church knew about my predicament and they were also a wonderful support system around the children and me.

Through the leading of God, they tapped into my gift of singing. And for seven years, I made myself unconditionally available to the church's Music Ministry. I sang wherever and whenever I was asked. How could I say "no" to something that made me feel so accomplished and fulfilled? I loved singing very much and saw many people blessed, healed, and delivered. Singing unto the Lord had become my life! My children and grandmother were such troupers and supported me in my quest to fulfill purpose. Granny, who lived with us at the time, never complained she just went about taking care of the family as though she gave birth to all of us. I really depended on her in every way, shape, and form. No one could ever take her place.

My children were great. They never complained either, at least I never heard them. They were obedient and compliant even when there were demands placed on their lives. Their compliance made life so much less complicated for me. It was as though the Lord was also making them into vessels of honor. It became abundantly clear that we were meant to do exploits for the Lord. Granny's prayers were not in vain. Our task would be to bring "good news" to those who were downtrodden.

I was going through some of the worst trials of my life, but God still used me to serve those in worse conditions. Sometimes it was hard to keep up with the demands of church, work, and family. But I knew that staying involved in church activities would keep me from succumbing to the pressures that were surrounding me. I had to endure moments of hopelessness and anxiety. My heart would race so fast it felt like it could jump out of my chest. Yet somehow, by "divine intervention" I would feel calm and resilience enabling me to rise again and face another challenge.

It never dawned on me back then that the Lord was actually preparing me for ministry. I was being molded into the vessel of honor He predestined me to be. The more time I spent at His feet, the stronger I became in

Him. A special bond of love was being formed as His Word became very personal to me. It was as though He was sharing His deepest thoughts with me. In His presence I felt no condemnation, only love. It was like crawling up in His lap where I felt so secure. I knew that no hurt or pain could touch me there.

I was being trained in service for my Lord. I just didn't know to what magnitude. The Lord began to guide me, first to join the choir and then to teach Sunday school. However, every Sunday morning was a challenge to get me and my three children to church on time. Especially because I didn't own a car and we had to take the bus. Thank God for compassionate and understanding leaders who are led by the Holy Spirit. They were so kind and understanding even when I had difficulty with my schedule. I was determined to get through it and the only way to come out victorious was to be involved in the Kingdom. The youth in my class were "on fire" for the Lord, and the Sister who assisted me was anointed in worship unto God. It blessed me to be in their company every Sunday morning.

One of my greatest discoveries was finding out that prayer is the key. Somehow, I knew it would benefit me to be involved with various prayer activities such as "all night prayer." My sister, who brought me to Christ, played a vital role in my involvement with this group. She was a praying and fasting wonder! How I wished for the stamina and the fortitude that she displayed.

We would begin fasting on Friday and continue straight through until Sunday. We also met at the church on Friday nights to pray until Saturday morning. Invariably, there would be a mighty move of God in the church on Sunday. To God be the glory! What a blessing to have been a participant. God always responds to united prayer and fasting. Although sometimes it seemed like I was getting nowhere, I persevered, because I was desperate to become what God wanted me to be.

Chapter 5

My Conversion, My Call

*****The Lord hath called me from the womb; from the bowels of my mother hath he made mention of my name- Isaiah 49:1b**** (KJV)*

Once I received the Holy Spirit, I was so crazy in love with Jesus and so excited about this new life style. I rushed to the studio at my first opportunity to let the producer know that it was over. How could I go through with my former plans when the old me was gone? Imagine the look of disbelief on his face when I told him my decision. He was quite disappointed and amazed that I was willing to throw away such an opportunity. I wanted so desperately to leave the past behind that it did not even occur to me that I could have used the contract to record the brand new songs I was now singing unto God. Unfortunately, I did not even have guidance on how to fit this recording opportunity into my new lifestyle.

It all began when I visited Pentecostal Tabernacle in 1972. My sister Beverly, who was and still is a very persuasive lady, invited me to her church. The first service that I attended was quite boring in my opinion. But, my sister and her new friends would not give up on me. After weeks of constant pressure, they finally succeeded in convincing me to try again, and after that day I have never been the same.

It is strange how we sometimes run away from the very thing that will liberate us. I was one of those people who pretended that I was doing well on the outside, but on the inside, I felt like I was dying. By the age of 19, I already had three children, so there was a great demand on my life. I also was in a very abusive marriage and my life was empty. Jesus heard my cry for help, and no matter how hard I tried to run away from him, it was my destiny to come to know Him.

One Sunday evening in June of that year, my children and their nanny accompanied me over to my sister's house. I had no intentions of going to church that evening and even though I was not dressed "appropriately," that did not hinder my sister from posing the question as soon as I entered the living room. She would not accept "no" for an answer and sent the nanny to my house to get my one and only appropriate dress.

In the meantime, I actually hid underneath her bed hoping to frustrate her efforts of convincing me to go to church. I was convinced that I was not ready to make such a commitment. My baby daughter, Michelle, joined in search for Mommy and quite soon discovered my place of hiding. I emerged amidst laughter and teasing and was quite embarrassed and flustered. So, off to Church we went. My heart was racing and there was a marked difference between this gathering and the previous one I attended.

The preacher Eric Taylor, delivered a rather vibrant message that really touched my heart. The choir sang, "I'd Rather Have Jesus than Anything This World Affords Today." Immediately something began to take place in my entire (being). The flowing tears and my shaking body were clear signs that the ministry that night had impacted me more than I could explain. I began to experience overwhelming conviction about anything and everything that I could have ever done against the laws of God. I had experienced the Lord at a young age, but this was entirely different. This was definitely on another level and I felt like control of my life was being taken out of my hands. I felt a compulsion to release everything; all of my mistakes, disappointments, abuses, lies, pretenses, frustrations and heart break into the hands that were reaching out to me.

Something or Someone had gotten a hold of me and I wept at the altar that night in total repentance and sub-mission unto the Lord. I also received the Baptism of the Holy Spirit as evidenced by speaking in a language that no one on earth had ever taught me. What a beautiful experience that was! It still amazes me how God can transform a life in such a manner. *"And they were all filled with the Holy Ghost and began to speak with other tongues, as the Spirit gave them utterance; Then Peter said unto them, Repent, and be baptized every one of you in the Name of Jesus Christ for the remission of sins and ye shall receive the gift of the Holy Ghost -Acts 2:4, 38 (KJV).*

I lived in darkness for a long time and suddenly I came to **THE LIGHT**! My transformation was quite remarkable. Who can adequately explain a change from the inside out? It was a 180 degree turn for the better. I never felt anything like this before. I had a hunger for all that was pure, holy, good and true. I was willing to make any sac-rifice necessary to be what God wanted me to be.

Twenty-two years of living in sin left such deep wounds and scars in my life. I needed the Lord to heal me and make me a brand new creature. Outward changes were not as challenging once I yielded my life completely to Him. My life was rearranged. I knew, beyond the shadow of a doubt, that this was what I had been missing. My soul cried out with a willingness to do anything that would make me look like, act like, sound like, and smell like a true Christian.

A fire began to burn inside me. It motivated me to share this brand new experience with anyone willing to listen. No wonder the "Samaritan woman at the well" took off running through the streets of her city shouting, "come see a man who has told me everything about myself, this must be the Christ" (John 4:30). What a relief she must have experienced when she realized that Jesus was not just an ordinary man who had stopped by to flirt with her; but rather He wanted to converse with her as a real person and not as some piece of property to conquer and own. Not only that, He was a Jew and the Jews had no dealings with the Samaritans at that time.

Oh, what a love—the Love of Jesus! He broke down the middle wall of partition and began to minister to her. "For He is our peace, who hath made both one, and hath broken down the middle wall of partition between us" (Ephesians 2:14). After He told her about herself, He showed her the Way to eternal life. He explained to her how to make the necessary changes in her life. He affirmed her. He motivated her to leave the past behind and embrace a new future. The odds were against her; she was a woman and a Samaritan. What she saw in His eyes gave her the courage she needed to drink of the "Living Water." He did the same for me that night in 1972, and I have never stopped drinking from the "Wells of Salvation!"

Missions – The Whisper

After about four or five years later, something tremendous took place. During a Missions Service, the pastor preached with fervent anointing. As usual, the Missions Department presented a program that softened my heart and compelled me to totally commit myself to the Lord and His service. I thought I was doing well, but when the word of God came forth, I realized that there was so much more to be done. We needed to bring men, women and children to a saving knowledge of Jesus Christ. I started to weep and could not stop. What a place to be in! I really don't quite remember how I got home from church that day. I just knew that I was very weak after weeping and pouring out my soul to the Lord. Somehow I made it to church that night and sang in the choir, but I knew then that I would never be the same again.

I started having dreams about becoming a missionary. I remember one dream distinctly. I was teaching children under a tree in the back of a church building. I knew in my dream that I was not in Jamaica. I pondered this in my heart, waiting for an explanation or the fulfillment of the dream.

I had been brought up religiously by my grandmother. She was a prayer warrior and would wake up early in the morning, often as early as 4:00 AM. She would talk to God and call out our names to Him. Sometimes I would be so scared when she would call my name to the Lord, that I would become frozen in the position that I was laying. Wishing that she would pick someone else's name because I could literally feel the flames of hell! Of course, I only had these experiences when I felt that I had yielded to youthful temptations the day before and did not have a chance to confess and repent.

Most of the time it made me feel good to know that God was listening to Granny's prayers and that I was included. I firmly believe that the hand of God was upon my life from those early days of childhood. Obviously, there was a call on my life and I was being chosen for a special work!

The Dawning of A New Day!

*After the **CALL**, an awakening occurred in me and a shift began to take place in my mindset- I was no longer afraid of my first husband anymore. The physical, emotional, psychological and economic abuses, the shame and embarrassment that accompany domestic violence no longer held me bound. Decades of allowing others to torment and malign me as a result of my low self image (Pauline=small) had worn me down, and yet, developed a deep desire to discover myself. The revelation came with a passion to begin nurturing my true identity in Christ and it was at that time* *that I made a decision to do the one thing that would release me from my first earthly husband's control. I divorced him (he is now deceased). In my new found freedom, I fell into the arms of my true First Husband (Isaiah 54:5; Hosea 2:11-KJV). This choice brought a new revelation of my real friends and circle of support. It also exposed my religious acquaintances who continue to judge me for my decision to this day! In spite of all that, I continued to move forward with my life. I stood on Romans 8:1(KJV) - "There is therefore no condemnation to those who are in Christ Jesus; who walk not after the flesh but after the Spirit."*

In my gratefulness I would have done what one woman did as depicted in the gospels. We're told of the time when Jesus was anointed with the very best ointment. It was worth one year's wages. *In Matthew 26:6 –7 'Now when Jesus was in Bethany, in the house of Simon the leper, there came unto Him a woman having an alabaster box of very precious ointment, and poured it on His head, as* He *sat at meat' and Mark 14:3 'And being in Bethany in the house of Simon the leper, as He sat at meat, there came a woman having an alabaster box of ointment of spikenard very precious; and she brake the box, and poured it on His head'* We see where the ointment was poured out on His head. The accounts of Luke and John show how His feet were anointed both with the precious spikenard from the alabaster box and the tears of the woman who then wiped them with her hair. In all four accounts (of the same event) we see how angry the disciples became. They saw such acts of worship as wasteful and unnecessary.

It is disheartening to think that the disciples spent so much time observing their Master's lifestyle and still lacked spiritual sensitivity.

There is no mention in the scriptures of the woman being intimidated by the criticism. She was not hindered in any way. She willingly gave her very best sacrificial praise. Jesus received her offering with true love and forgiveness. The disapproval of the self-righteous men could not prevent this display of love. He did not judge the woman but rather vehemently applauded the very act. He said in St. John 12:7..."Let her alone: against the day of my burying hath she kept this." This time, he was sitting among a few friends and his disciples, but among them, he still had enemies. As the fragrance of her sacrifice filled the room, Jesus was criticized for allowing her to even touch Him. But, He knew that she was fulfilling her purpose.

Before she had her encounter with Him she was dead inside. Life had no meaning and she was sick of her life-style. She needed a change. The men used and abused her and the women hated and shunned her. Jesus saw her as a precious treasure. This act of worship proved that she had come to her senses and was in her right mind. She heeded the call and worshipped Him unashamedly. I have done the same and cast my life that was in shambles, at His feet. He did not turn me away or scorn me. He never told me that I was not clean enough to come into His presence. Instead, every time that I came to Him, He embraced me and just bathed my heart with His love. He healed me as he was unfolding a purpose in my life. His touch transformed my life and made me a true worshipper of Him, the one true God. And as I worship Him, He anoints me and there is sweet fragrance that fills this house.

The change taking place in my life could also be seen on my children. I wanted them to have the same experiences in the Lord that I was having. I never entertained the thought of them being too young to make a commitment to Him. The church where I belonged had no restrictions on children getting saved. Although I did not know a lot about the book of Deuteronomy at that time, or about the laws God set forth to parents, there was something in my heart that began to instruct me on how to raise my children. I took them to prayer meetings and Bible Study. I still remember them sleeping on top of, and underneath, the benches in the church. No one had to persuade me, I just knew immediately that I wanted them to share in whatever was responsible for making this awesome transformation in my life.

Chapter 6

Henry's Call - The Way We Met

whom He called........them He also glorified
Romans 8:30 (KJV)

In 1977, a change began to take place in a young man's life. Henry was the youngest of three boys, and Catholic by religion. He served as an altar boy in the Catholic Church from age 12 to 16. His father desired him to become a priest. He did, but not of the order that his father would have chosen. Instead, he became a part of **THE ROYAL PRIESTHOOD** (I Peter 2:9). His change came when his older brother, Donovan, became converted at Pentecostal Tabernacle.

Music was Henry's passion. While still in High School, he played the bass guitar in a Reggae band. They performed at the Fountain Club just outside of Kingston, Jamaica. The band members played at the club until wee hours of the morning. That was his lifestyle for only a short while.

Henry was not satisfied with his life. There was a longing in his heart for something more meaningful. He was miserable and began to have conflicts with the manager of the club. He worked hard on those weekends but was not getting fair wages. No wonder the scripture declares the wages of sin is death (Romans 6:23). He felt like he was dying a slow death.

Around this time, Henry's brother Donovan started a crusade for his soul. Donovan had found such joy and peace in his new found faith that he could hardly wait for Henry to experience it. This noble gesture only angered his brother. As far as Henry knew, he was quite fine being a Catholic. He resented his brother for preaching to him about being saved. Because of the conflicts, the brothers grew apart for a while. Donovan drew wisdom from God in the form of a question for Henry. He asked him, "What is the name of your God?" Henry was quite astonished by the question, and after pausing and thinking about it, he responded quite adamantly, "God!"

Needless to say, the brothers entered into a deep and passionate discussion since Donovan had found an open door to witness. Henry received the word as it brought him to a realization of his ignorance pertaining to God. He did not have a personal relationship with Him. He did not even know His name.

He was like the Athenians referred to in Acts 19 who erected the stone with the inscription, "To The Unknown God." When the conversation ended, Henry decided that it was time for him to get to know this God for himself.

For the first time in his life, he actually knelt by his bed and prayed to God calling on the Name, Jesus. As he recalls, it was quite scary as the very presence of the Lord came into the room. He had never had such a visitation and did not know what to expect, so he quickly said, "goodnight Jesus!" He then pulled the covers over his head. Although exhausted, he was very enlightened and fell asleep as God prepared him for his next encounter.

One Sunday morning when he was returning home from a gig at the Fountain Club, the Lord helped him make a 180-degree turn. He was tired and not well dressed, but he had an appointment with God, that he had to keep. As the bus reached his stop, everything came to a halt for what seemed like an eternity. It was God again, and this time He was doing the talking. He told Henry not to get off at that stop because He was taking him to church. The bus remained at the stop, even though no one got off and no one got on. Everything was at a standstill to enable Henry to have this discourse with God, and as soon as it was over, the bus continued on its journey. Henry was not about to argue with God and so he consented. That morning Henry found himself at his brother's church. He was being ushered into a deeper encounter with this God in the Name of Jesus.

As he walked through the doors of the church he saw the strangest sight. There were people with their hands raised and crying as a brother from the church sang, "His Eye is on the Sparrow." He later found out that they were worshipping God using the name, Jesus. He could not understand why these people were crying yet they looked so happy. He soon learned that crying was a way these church people expressed "thank you" to this wonderful God. It was quite overwhelming for Henry, as their worship captured his attention like nothing ever did before. When he looked into their eyes, he saw hope. He knew he needed that hope, but did not know how to get it?

He decided to visit the church again. It was a Sunday evening and they were having an evangelistic service. He didn't know it then, but the enemy of his soul, (the flesh) tried to hinder him. A feeling of gross tiredness came over him and he fell into a deep sleep that almost caused him to miss the service. But his brother Donovan became proactive and rescued him from this blanket of discouragement. He was not in a good mood when he woke up and promptly told his brother that he changed his mind. Donovan persisted in his encouragement. He had some more "words of wisdom." He asked another pertinent question, "Do you love Jesus?" That did it! It was like a thousand jolts of electricity went through Henry, who would not be outdone. When Donovan said "prove it by going to church!" Henry squared his shoulders like a man and off they went. That Sunday night in March 1977 was the night Henry started his journey to walk hand-in-hand with Jesus. The service may have been just another evangelistic service to others, but to Henry it was the night his life changed forever.

This church was usually very well attended, and this night was no different. The pews were all filled and finding a seat was very difficult but God chose even the seat that Henry was to sit in that night. The ushers offered him a seat by an elderly lady who encouraged him to respond to the appeal to come forward and accept Jesus as his Savior and Lord. Everything was in place as God orchestrated it to be; and before it was all over, Henry was filled with the precious gift of the Holy Ghost speaking in tongues as the spirit gave him utterance. Then he was baptized in the name of Jesus Christ for the remission of his sins. He left the service that night beaming and glowing from his new faith in Jesus.

The first few weeks of his conversion were filled with obstacles and tests that could have destroyed him. One night, he actually yielded to the temptation to go back to the Reggae band and play at the club. God said, "I will never leave you or forsake you." So God, being true to His word, showed up with him that night and everything went wrong. Henry was not able to play the guitar. This was a true sign to him that God was also a God of love, mercy, and compassion. That night Henry vowed never to look back but to hold fast to God's unchanging hands. Another test that he faced was with his parents. His dad told him that if he kept up "this spirit thing", he would have to find somewhere else to live. His very life was even threatened as he tried to share his faith with the rest of the family.

God was developing this young man, preparing him for the day that we would meet. He had no idea what challenges were awaiting him. He was being prepared for a 'Goliath' situation and certainly needed the valiance and courage of David. I later learned that he developed an interest in me after becoming a part of the church. At the time of his conversion, my sisters and I would sing together in various services. Before we were formally introduced, Henry told me he would be so moved whenever I would get up to sing because of the strong anointing on my life.

He shared with me later that one night while he was going through a difficult time, although he came to church, he did not want to worship God. He decided to just be a spectator and not a participant. Henry was about to learn another lesson that night. He found out that he was no match for the Lord! God's manifested presence in the service caused such an avalanche of praise and worship that no one could hinder. I sang a solo that night. The song might have been, "When I look back and see where He's brought me from". He told me how he desperately tried to hold his ground in the balcony of the church with his arms folded as if that would stop the flow of God's presence from within. Well as I sang, God poured out his anointing and Henry danced all over the balcony that night. The anointing really destroys the yoke! (Isaiah 10:27)

It would be safe to say that because of our involvement in our church's Music Department, it was inevitable that we would discover each other. He played in the band and I sang in the choir. We both lived in the same area of Kingston, and sometimes traveled together on public transportation or rode with one of the brothers from the church.

A brother from the church was so impressed with the way Henry played the guitar that he bought him his first and very own acoustic guitar. It was also through this same brother that we started to interact more closely. He suggested that we form a trio. Soon after forming the trio, a chorale was also formed. I sang lead and Henry played the lead guitar. Of course, this brought us even closer. We began to sing at other churches, at promotions for events at church, and participated in various other projects. One of these was the church's first 'long playing record,' a 33 1/3-rpm record entitled, "Praises from Pentecostal Tabernacle." Henry played the guitar for the solos that I performed on the record.

If the young people went on a hike, we would somehow end up walking together and I began to find him quite interesting and amusing as he began to make up the silliest songs about anything that he could identify along the way, while he played his brand-new guitar. He was a lot of fun and I needed that in my life. Henry told me later that, it was during these times that the Lord would impress upon his heart that I was to be his wife. Whenever we got together for rehearsal, I would begin to sense a change in him, a change that made me feel absolutely out of control. I felt like he was looking into my soul and that I had become involuntarily transparent before him. I did not feel violated; it was more like a warm covering was placed over me and suddenly, I felt so protected.

Finally, one night he mustered up enough courage to lean on his acoustic guitar, and with the widest eyes and widest grin, he told me that he was in love with me. I laughed until I thought I would pass out. Well, guess what, the laugh was on me, because it happened. Our close acquaintances began to tease me about my "friend." I would get so annoyed and rebuke them for what they said. My mind was only focused on the new horizons God had in store for me.

Later when the children and I left Jamaica, the choir and band members came to bid us farewell at the airport. This was the usual practice for those who had served in one capacity or another in the church. Henry was there but I avoided him and would deliberately not look his way because of my mixed feelings. Many years later he expressed to me, that as raindrops fell to the ground and the airplane took off, tears fell from his eyes. He was hurting so badly, and he didn't quite know what to do. But, he vowed that "anywhere you are, I'll find you" and he made good on that promise.

Chapter 7

Life in the USA

****I will instruct thee and teach thee in the way which
thou shalt go: I will guide thee with mine eye
-Psalm 32:8 (KJV)****

M ama had migrated to the United States in 1966
and finally filed immigration papers for my children and I to follow in her footsteps. So, in June 1979,
after a long waiting period for our visas, our migration
to the US took place. We were no longer at the mercy of
The Jamaican Embassy. Instead, the captain of the aircraft was announcing our arrival at the John F. Kennedy
International Airport and Mama was waiting with arms
wide open. Finally we were in the USA together. Mama,
thank you for paving the way and setting the pace!

A brand new start- land of opportunity

I couldn't wait to embark on my new way of life even
though I did experience being homesick for Jamaica.
However, when I called the church and heard a familiar
voice, it instantly lifted my spirits. The Lord continued
to watch over me in Staten Island, NY and did extraordinary things just to reiterate that He would never leave

me nor forsake me. One of these significant moments took place when I traveled to Manhattan to look for work. It was a journey, which could have been my last. I should have known the day would have been challenging when I burned my hand as I fried some bologna for breakfast.

I had to take a ferryboat from Staten Island, then a subway train to get to where my interview was scheduled. Before I boarded the train there was a Muslim gentleman who motioned for me to stand beside him. I tried to ignore him but he followed me onto the train, and he got off at the same stop I did. I didn't know it then, but God was going to use him to save my life.

Manhattan sometimes has gusty winds and this was one of those times. I was trying to focus on finding the Employment Office while being distracted by the man who was still following me. I didn't realize what happened until it was over. As I was walking, an entire windowpane came loose from a building and crashed right beside me. It would have landed on my head, but God prompted this same man who was following me, to pull me back seconds before it landed. I was so shaken that my legs felt like jelly. Many people have died in Manhattan because of "freak" accidents like that, and I had come close to being one of them.

Similarly, three people were killed in Chicago while driving by a skyscraper. This was due to high winds which caused the scaffolding to come loose and land on top of the cars they were in. I know that God gave me a miracle that day in Manhattan, but it was not the only one I was to receive.

Another incident occurred around October 1980 while I was on the Staten Island ferry. I was on my way to work in Manhattan and was traveling with a new friend from my neighborhood. These boats can accommodate a large number of people and it was usually jam-packed. We wanted to be the first to exit the boat so we positioned ourselves at the top of a stairwell. What happened next could have been fatal, but God stepped in right on time. The compass was not working and the current just took the boat completely off course. The boat hit the piling instead of the docking resulting in a violent impact. When I opened my eyes I was upside down on top of the other people who had also been hurled down the stairs. My friend landed not too far from me and was injured in the fall. We saw blood and began to scramble to safety to see where this blood was coming from.

My right arm felt strange and when I looked, I saw that it had swollen to approximately twice its size. However, the blood was not coming from me; it was coming from my friend, whose shin had a big gash across it. Within moments, the place was in pandemonium. There were cameras flashing and many people talking to me all at once. We were then put into an ambulance and taken to St. Vincent's Hospital. I had suffered a sprain in my right wrist from which a ganglion cyst developed. The accident was in the evening news and I saw my face flashing all across the papers and on television. I didn't want to be a celebrity that badly and certainly not at that price. The Lord healed my wrist over time and today there is no sign of any damage done. Praise the Lord!

The children and I began to adjust to our new way of life. Church, school and work were established and each component came with its own set of challenges. For my children, the challenge was mostly in the way they dressed. I couldn't afford to buy Andrew popular sneakers; in fact, the ones he owned were an inexpensive off-brand. I didn't know this at the time but, he didn't go to school for a week because he couldn't stand being teased about his shoes. Charmaine and Michelle faced a challenge in their gym class because I only allowed them to wear skirts. I wanted to bring them up in the way we started back home.

At times it was hard, especially living at home with Mama and my other sisters. I knew they didn't mean any harm, but they tried to persuade me to comply with their standards and to convince me that I was too hard on the girls. Maybe I was too strict, but I was determined that they would stay in the church and be upstanding young people, making a difference wherever they would go. I endured, since I was certain that what I was doing was right for my children.

Just before I left Jamaica, the pastoral counsel was, "Nevertheless, whereto you have already attained, walk by the same rule, mind the same thing" (Philippians 3:16). I was determined to walk by the same rules and mind the same things. Sometimes I fell down, but I got right back up again and kept on walking.

When I came to the United States, I was in for a rude awakening as far as holiness standards were concerned. I began to see church in a different light. My perspectives changed. Methods may change and some adjustments may become necessary, but thank God, His message remains the same. What one does and how it is done will speak volume about one's character. I learned that a real relationship with Christ is paramount in maintaining a way of life that is pleasing to Him. There is just no way to circumvent that. We must be totally sold to the cause of Christ and be willing to go on the Potter's wheel and be made over day-by-day in order to be the vessel of honor that He desires us to be.

Before I left home, one of the elder deacons told me that if I proceeded to migrate to the United States, things were going to get pretty rough. I had faced so many challenges that were unprecedented in just two short years that I began to reflect on what the elder had said. His words had put fear in my heart. But this fear only made me arm myself for the battles to come. I still believe that "...greater is He that is in you than he that is in the world". (1 John 4:4) I also know that, "God has not given us a spirit of fear, but of power and of love and of a sound mind" (2 Timothy 1:7). I may lose a battle now and then but through Christ I had already won the war.

When I look back and see how far I've come, I do not regret moving to the US. Today, we are chasing after God with everything we have. Our desire is to know Him in a way we've never known Him before. We may differ on methods, but we strive to forget the things which are behind us, and are pressing to fulfill His will for our individual lives.

In 1981, a Pastor from St. Alban's, Queens, New York invited me and my children to join his church and for me to join the choir. So, my children and I moved from Staten Island to Queens, New York. We were members of this church for approximately three years. During our time at Oneness Pentecostal Tabernacle, I was a part of a trio who eventually made a recording. My two girls, Charmaine and Michelle, sang with the junior trio and my son Andrew played the drums. Our singing became recognized at this church and we were especially blessed when the family was asked to minister together.

Once we moved to Queens, I began to pursue a degree in nursing. It was my mother's dream for me to become a nurse. Since I loved people anyway, I thought, "why not?" I completed my pre-nursing courses and was accepted into the nursing program at Queensborough Community College (QCC).

I was so desperate to know God's will for my life. He was drawing me into a deeper relationship with Him. The **call of God** from years before was gripping me. I was so hungry for more involvement in the Kingdom and I did not want to fail the Lord. I needed a change; I was tired of the status quo. "O God," I prayed, "remember me in my afflictions. Do not turn your back on me." I was also being pursued by some of the single brothers in the church. This motivated me to go on a two-week consecration of prayer and fasting to find the mind of God for my children and me

I really needed a mentor or a father figure here on earth, someone I could trust. I was in a chasm of loneliness and it was an awful place to be. I became very depressed. I tried to balance home, church and school but it was very difficult. It was as though I was in a state of isolation and hopelessness. When I was around people I'd show them my best on the outside. Meanwhile on the inside I felt like I was being held hostage in a deep, dark dungeon. I was being oppressed by evil thoughts that would constantly try to envelope my mind. I felt bound by the ugly chains of doubt, fear, and frustration. But, whenever I focused on Him, the Lord would gently wrap His arms around me to let me know that He was still with me. I would feel His presence so strong, as the Psalmist David said, "Yea though I walk through the valley of the shadow of death, I will fear no evil, for thou art with me; thy rod and thy staff they comfort me..." (Psalm 23:4). In order to overcome these experiences, I commanded my soul to keep hungering and thirsting after His righteousness.

One night I called the children into my bedroom and told them that I was inviting them to go on a fast with me. I explained to them that Mommy needed a companion. Well, they didn't blink an eye; they just sort of stared at me. We decided that we would do a 24-hour fast and wait to see what God would do for us. We didn't invite anyone else to join us. I didn't think they would understand the magnitude of my desperation to know the mind of God in this matter. Sometimes, one has to meet the Lord alone. Sweet communion and fellowship can be experienced as we embark on that one on one with Him. I did not sense any resistance from the children, so there was no need to exclude them. We had become one in spirit. The outcome would definitely affect them too. We fasted and prayed together and then it was a time of waiting to see what God would do.

I kept seeking the Lord for direction and I expected the Lord to speak to me and show me the way. Well, He did and it was not easy, for the word was from Micah 4:10, "Be in pain, and labor to bring forth, O daughter of Zion, like a woman in travail; for now shall thou go forth out of the city, and thou shall dwell in the field, and thou shall go even to Babylon; there shall thou be delivered; there the Lord shall redeem thee from the hand of thine enemies." Whoa! Lord that is not exactly what I wanted to hear. I'm looking for a reprieve, not more travailing. That is more hard work, why me? But that was the response I received.

I needed help to determine the right direction for my family. I received an invitation to join a ministry in Canada and in Upstate New York. I thought hard and prayed about it, but didn't feel a release in my spirit to go to either place.

My question was still, "Lord, where in the world are we going to go? The city could be New York, but where is the field?" By then I had decided that He wasn't going to send us out by ourselves, but there would be a "head" to whom I would yield and the Lord would show him the way. Remember what the Lord did with Abraham. Well, He was bringing an Abraham my way. I had laughed like Sarah, (Abraham's wife) laughed, but the joke was on me. Henry Abraham Brash was being prepared to take up a challenge of a lifetime. He was like David being equipped to take on Goliath. He was to be my wedded husband and to become a father to children entering adolescence. Sometimes what God allows just does not make sense. He had no prior experience in marriage or in fatherhood. To the natural eye, it didn't seem possible that such a relationship could work.

I poured my energies into helping build individuals in Christ. It was quite encouraging to go to church on a Sunday morning and see the familiar faces of those I knew from Jamaica. Oftentimes requests would be made for me to sing someone's favorite song that I used to sing back at PenTab. As the songs rang out, hands would be raised in praise unto our God and the tears would begin to flow. It was so reassuring to experience the same sweet flow of the anointing, as He would sweep throughout the congregation. The anointing truly destroys the yoke!

We experienced many phenomenal manifestations of the presence of God. I recall one event where I felt led of the Holy Spirit to sing the old hymn, "It is well with my soul". I was obedient and sang the song. What happened next was purely the Lord's doing and it was marvelous in our sight. It has made a definite impression in my mind. A young woman who was visiting for the first time began to weep. Before anyone could get to her, she began to crawl on her hands and knees, down the aisle all the way to the altar. While I kept on singing; the prayer warriors and altar workers immediately went over and began to minister to her. She was transformed that day as the Lord gloriously filled her with the Holy Spirit. Just a few weeks later, I felt led to sing this song again. Again, I watched as a woman began to weep right in her seat. After just a few short moments, she was transformed as she received her personal Pentecost that day. But after the singing and the fellowshipping was over, there we were again, just the four of us. The children and I would sit around the dining table and recount the significant happenings in each service.

The children were growing up, and new challenges kept coming with such intensity that sometimes I would become so overwhelmed. I can truly say that even in the midst of each trial, it was the Spirit of God that kept us and we refused to let go of His promises.

I tried my best to maintain a godly home, and to teach them the principles of the Word of God and what it meant to "grow" in the Lord. I know that I did not do everything right, but I am very grateful that today they still love and serve the Lord and are teaching their children to do the same. Then it happened. I began to feel a yearning for someone on my level to share my hopes and dreams with. I needed someone who I could trust. There were so many acquaintances but after making a few futile attempts and discovering their ulterior motives, I had to sever the relationships.

One night at a Youth Rally being held at my church, a mutual friend casually told me that "Brash" was in the States. He was attending Bible School at Jackson College of Ministries (JCM). Out of curiosity, I called him. He was in the school cafeteria at that time. At first, he did not recognize my voice since we had not communicated on the telephone since I moved to the United States.

After the small talk ended, he wasted no time telling me he had never stopped loving me. Henry was and still is a pursuer. If he received a vision of a good thing, he would find a way to possess it. How was I to know that things could develop from just one telephone call? I was in total shock. Something made me hold on and keep right on talking. Of course, the scripture that I had received after the fast was still on my mind.

I was very curious to see how he was doing and to find out what his plans were for the summer. He told me that a pastor in Mississippi had offered to teach him to fly an airplane. After talking with me, he decided that he would rather spend his summer in New York. He declined the pastor's offer but years later he had the opportunity to fly a plane while we lived in Pittsburgh, PA. "Thank you Jesus, hallelujah, amen". There were several young people from Pentecostal Tabernacle in Jamaica, who were now living around the five Boroughs in New York City. I knew they would enjoy the fellowship of *Henry and his guitar, for old times' sake.* I began

to make preparations for his visit and I waited in anticipation for his arrival. There were many pleasant memories about 'home' that filled my mind and I could hardly
wait to see him. He had completed two years of training
at the Caribbean Bible Institute (CBI) in Jamaica and
approximately two years at Jackson College of Ministries
(JCM) in Jackson, Mississippi. I longed to hear of his
experiences.

Henry had two things going for him: he had known
my children from when they were younger and they were
impressed with his guitar playing. As a matter of fact,
they found him quite intriguing. Watching him play the
guitar and dance before the Lord can only be likened to
the time when David danced as the Ark of the Covenant
was being brought back into Israel. The anointing would
be so strong that he would literally let go of the guitar
in the air and the band members would have to reach
out and catch it. He still plays the guitar but when the
anointing comes, he "plays" with the understanding. He
plays the keyboard the most now and the Lord uses
him mightily in the psalmist ministry. When he leads
worship during our church services, there is a definite
shift in the spirit. We know that we have entered into
the very presence of the Lord. It is the most awesome
experience!

From the moment Henry came to New York, we began
to minister together. My prayers began to change. We
would visit the sick and spend a lot of time just singing
together and planning a future which we had never dis-
cussed before. We were trying to understand what the
Lord was doing in us. All of a sudden my life did not seem
so dull anymore. I had found something that appealed
to me more than anything in this world. I started to feel
a sweet peace and consolation sweep over me. But, I
needed much faith and grace to endure the comments
from people who did not share our vision. During his
visit, he was invited to preach at several churches and

also at our local assembly. I was amazed at how God had developed this young man.

In Ecclesiastes 3:1 the Bible states, "To everything there is a season, and a time to every purpose under the heaven." It was not long after Henry arrived in New York that we realized there was something special happening. I cannot explain it, but even when it appeared to me that a relationship between us would be impossible and impractical, it was as though God was bonding us together for a special ministry, and a sweet peace would engulf us.

He showed me a gentleness that was quite becoming of a good Christian man. After the abrasive relationships that I had encountered, this was like the calm after the storm. Something wonderful was happening in my life. I felt hope against hope. I was falling in love with him; but since I had never felt love like this before in any human relationship, I was not sure. I was mixed up inside, and was worried about what people would say. God had definitely taken us to another level and was doing a new thing in our lives. Together we began to bask in Him. It was as though everyone else was blocked out just for a moment, and we were the only two people that existed. But, reality was waiting!

All the events in my life so far had been quite unpredictable, but this was bigger and this was different. At times it seemed like the odds were against us. I have found that even when we are doing the will of God, we will be tested. Someone said, 'this test is your storm'. These storms are not meant to destroy us, but rather to strengthen our faith in Him and to reinforce that which is good and right for us.

We'll only know if we have done His will at the end of that trial. It is a process that we must go through to be perfected and fit for use in God's kingdom. I would remember the scripture, Romans 8:31 "What shall we then say to these things, if God be for us, who can be against us". With such consolation, we began to move forward in our relationship.

I knew that Henry and I ministered well together and there was a strong possibility that we could move forward in that ministry as a family. Henry had bright hopes and dreams for us as a family. We talked about moving to Jackson, Mississippi, in order for him to complete Bible School. I didn't object to moving since I felt that the location did not matter. What mattered was that we were in the perfect will of God for our lives. I began to cry out to the Lord for Him to clarify for me what was taking place.

He did. Just a few months before, I had done a tour with the trio and there were plans being made for us to sing at the General Conference. Doors were opening for this ministry and I really enjoyed it. However, since I had just been away from my children for quite a while, I decided it would be unwise to leave again, so soon. My decision to stay home was not well received. It seemed to trigger a change in some of my relationships. I could not understand it, and I was hurt tremendously but I see now that God was still at work behind the scenes. It took some time for me to recover from the hurt and disappointment.

It's so important for Christian leaders to be sensitive to the needs of the unmarried and especially the single parents in their congregation. It is also imperative that these men and women seek and submit to ministries that function with compassion and integrity. Young men and women need mentorship as they make decisions regarding relationships and marriage. While there are many things to consider, I believe the first and most important issue should be their relationship with Christ. Compatibility in your faith is the best foundation to build on.

The Bible says, "how can two walk together except they agree?" Light has no part with darkness. We should not be unequally yoked together with unbelievers. We must believe the same thing, otherwise there will be major consequences down the road. When the spiritual foundation is laid and each has a real relationship with the Lord, they will be able to forge every storm, together. No wonder the Bible says that we should seek first the Kingdom of God and His righteousness and all 'these' things shall be added to you.

I was so caught up in my new relationship that I was oblivious to how people had changed around me. The final blow was when my children and I were told we were no longer welcome in the place we called our church home. I felt like the life had been snuffed out of me.

Rejection can be devastating and some do not recover from it. We did not camp out there but began to focus on a brighter day. We knew that the Lord would never forsake us. He already told us in His Word, fear only the one who can kill both body and soul. He gave me the boldness that I needed to meet this challenge. It broke my heart that I was not able to protect my children from that hurt. How could things have changed so drastically? But, people do change; and sometimes without realizing what they have done. I'm happy to report that today, Love and forgiveness have conquered all the hurts that were inflicted upon my family.

Shortly after Henry had come to New York, my mother told me, in a telephone conversation, that she had a vision of our wedding. I only mentioned Henry as a young man from Jamaica was coming to visit. Well, as we all love to add a little spice, I might have told her some years before that he was in love with me. In her vision, we were married in her home church.

All the struggles that we were encountering only served to intensify what we felt for each other. It was like a fire of determination burning between us. There were days when I thought I couldn't go on. My faith in the church was being tested, and sometimes I didn't quite know if I still believed. Henry had returned to Bible School, but something had changed in him. He was having a hard time financially. Someone actually made an offer to pay the tuition that he owed, but he had much to thank the Lord for because he did not accept the offer. This individual had ulterior motives that could have destroyed his testimony.

Before Henry went back to Bible School, he also faced the firing squad as he was told that he would never become anything worthwhile in the Kingdom. It was as if this man of God wanted to curse his life. We were both so confused and disillusioned at this point.

The Apostle Paul mentored the young brother Timothy and empowered him to become a vibrant minister of the gospel. The Prophet Elijah coached young Elisha and he received the double portion. Young Christian men and women need Elders to be there for them to coach them in the things of God.

Even though Henry's intentions were honorable, they were met with much resistance. He was being bombarded with statements that planted seeds of fear in his heart. Here he was, thinking that he was in the perfect will of God. For a short while he was in a state of confusion. Then he found out that phone calls were being made to several leaders in an attempt to destroy his reputation and ministry. He was like the modern day David, being pursued by Saul.

All he had going for him was his faith in a God who had provided a way for him to come to the United States of America. This kept him going, along with the fact that I was there waiting for him. It might sound crazy, but this increased our desire to be with each other. With mixed emotions, Henry left Bible School and came to New York to work and to save towards the wedding. We encouraged each other to the best of our ability. And the Lord never left us alone, he sent us people who encouraged us in our decision. They began to look far deeper than the natural eyes could see. This was, as one preacher said, a set-up for God to get His glory.

I recall how frail and vulnerable I was. I prayed and fasted more than ever, during that season of my life. Jesus was my dearest and closest friend, as He still is to this day. He came to my rescue so many times. It was as though He held me in his arms and comforted me. Was it worth it? Yes, if such a question was asked of the acorn that becomes the tall, strong oak tree or the grain of sand which eventually becomes the pearl. Well, I'd say, it was well worth it! He is the Friend of a wounded heart! And He makes all things work together for our good.

Chapter 8

Each for the Other, Both for the Lord

*'Therefore shall a man leave his father and his mother,
and shall cleave unto his wife and they
shall be one flesh"
Genesis 2:24'*

Sometimes the spirit of Daniel comes upon a child of God with a challenge for them to stand alone. But one realizes soon, that he is not alone, for Jesus goes with Him. We were married at Mama's church on December 24, 1983. It was cold outside, but inside we were safe and warm. Pictures were made and one dear friend even made a short film on an 8mm camera. We have since put it on video to preserve it.

My stepfather Pops drove me to the church and had to literally drive up onto the sidewalk in order for me to get inside the church safely. There was so much snow on the ground, but it was beautiful. Everything looked so pure and clean. My husband's sister and cousin came to represent his family. We couldn't afford to bring other family members from Jamaica but we did receive well wishes from those who couldn't attend, including his parents.

Friends came from far and near to celebrate this time with us. The best part was that I was able to get dressed in my mother's beautiful bedroom and walk down the long staircase with the flowing veil wafting around me. I felt brand new. It was as if I was in a dream.

Once we arrived at the church, anxiety set in. I realized that we were both taking a leap of faith. Our marriage would not have been accepted by our church in Jamaica. I was a divorced woman with three teenage children and there was a ten year difference in our age. To most people he was like David taking on Goliath. This precious young man was willing to become my husband, to love and to cherish me until death us do part. He never had any children of his own, but he was willing to come into this union and create a "blended" family situation for better or for worse. As I walked down the aisle the pianist played the song "Keeper of my heart." When I joined him at the altar we sang that song to each other. The blending of our voices was symbolic of the blending of our lives. There was a fusion taking place and we were being bonded together for the glory of God.

All along the way, as I begin to count my blessings I am convinced that we were meant for each other. God had everything arranged. He gave us free will and we used it. Even though our decision caused some concerns, we trusted God, held on to faith and we came through alright.

As Mama sang, "The Lord's Prayer," we wept in total submission to His will. A precious friend of mine sang, "The closer I get to you", the more you make me feel, God's given us such a love, and it has captured me". Then the entire wedding party stood and sang the chorus, "You are loved, you can risk loving me..."

Even though things didn't go exactly the way that we had planned, there was such consolation in my soul that I was doing the right thing. We let the Lord do the choosing for us. He always knows what's best for His children. We spent a lot of time in prayer and fasting and He came through for us. The love that Henry had to give was the purest of all. I knew within my heart that we would struggle at first just trying to balance this whole thing and getting the family relationship established. Without a doubt, I was standing on the promises of Proverbs 10:22 which declares that, "The blessing of the Lord, it maketh rich, and he addeth no sorrow with it!". Praise God, Hallelujah, thank you Jesus!

We had beaten the odds and were willing to make the necessary sacrifices to build our home with God's help and to keep our marriage and home intact. *Except the LORD build the house, they labour in vain that build it: except the LORD keep the city, the watchman waketh but* in *vain - Psalm 127:1(KJV)*. Sometimes God will ask us to do extraordinary things. It might not make sense to the natural man but that is the time when we must trust Him the most. Abram did not know where God was sending him and his family. However, he trusted Him and walked by faith. He left his homeland in search of a place whose builder and maker was God. That's implicit trust!

My Abraham left his birth home, came to a strange land with a hope and a prayer seeking after God. He experienced more challenges than he had bargained for. You may be going through a particular situation right now and feel like you have been forgotten. You may have many questions in your mind about the will of God and whether you are doing the right thing. Just know that if you follow the principles of the Bible, God will honor your decisions. The free will that you have been given is not for your own purpose. If you have accepted Christ in your life and are striving to maintain a real relationship with Him, He will mentor you. He is the Wonderful Counselor!

Before long, we had committed ourselves to assisting in a ministry in Massachusetts. What a journey! I can still see the five of us in the back of the truck with the furniture we were taking to Springfield, Massachusetts. After we unloaded our belongings off the truck, the children got back on and left for New York, where they would stay with my mother and stepfather for awhile. I cried and my heart broke for this was not how I intended it to happen. When I started the plans for moving to America, I was told to leave my children in Jamaica, while I worked in the US. I refused to take that suggestion but look what had happened to us. We were being separated, and there was nothing that I could do about it.

I cried also because we had been deceived. What we were promised, we did not receive. We had to move into an unfinished and dirty apartment. We were unable to communicate with our neighbors as there was a language barrier. I remember one entire week where we had no food to eat and we didn't know anyone in the area. We lived on hot chocolate all week until finally, Henry met a gentleman who was kind enough to speak to his wife and together they blessed us with a whole chicken. May God bless them wherever they are today! I know sometimes we all fail, but it was our endeavor to be good stewards of the responsibilities that God has put in our hands. As the song says:

'If I can help somebody as I pass along,
If I can cheer somebody with a word or song,
If I can show somebody that He's traveling wrong,
Then my living will not be in vain.

I immediately signed up to continue school. Since Henry was not a permanent resident, he couldn't work so he volunteered with the radio station on campus. We saw a lot of each other and we stayed in constant communication with Mama and the children. The children came to visit when they could. They were wonderful, although I'm sure they could tell that I had many fears and doubts regarding this giant decision that I had made. I felt so responsible for the disruption in their lives.

My mind was in a whirlwind. Yet, I held on to faith and faith works! The pastor who had promised faithfully to support us with housing and to assist Henry to get his papers had deceived us. Once again our faith was being tested. Everything turned out to be a farce. The church dismantled. God led us into another ministry. The church was called, "New Hope." Praise Jesus, we spent four wonderful months with that pastor and saints. That was like an oasis in the desert and our faith was renewed!

In those early days, marriage was a challenge. There was a lesson to be learned, we were different from one another. We didn't see things the same way all the time. I was accustomed to having the last word and could not accept someone else telling me what to do. I was used to the children praying together with me, and I tutored them in these sessions. They never questioned my decisions. In our culture children did what they were told, and without question.

He loved to play the guitar while praying and I sometimes just wanted to pray without that interference -that's how I saw it then. He would become caught up in his method but I could not "tap in." I did not realize it then, but I was unwittingly jealous of his time with the Lord. He was ministering to his God and Creator, and I was not understanding and actually trying to interfere with such a beautiful expression of worship. I hated it most when we would have an argument and he would pick up his guitar. Oh, I would get so mad. But, making up was always so beautiful. I could not stand hurting him and he felt the same way about me.

It is amazing how the Lord will form and fashion us even in all of our adversities. We ministered in song and word, and the pastor of New Hope mentored us as only God could have anointed him to do. He was quite blessed by our worship and music ministry and asked us to stay and work with them there. Even though this was a safe haven, we did not feel led to stay. Our next question was "What now Lord?"

With this "new hope" to hold on to, we were more determined now than ever to make our marriage work and to bring the family back together. We decided to go back to New York to regroup and formulate a plan for the future. We didn't take very long to make a decision which way to go. There was another pastor in Pittsburgh, Pennsylvania, whom we had supported in times past. Certainly, he would be good to us. After all, we were bringing gifts and talents to his church. We had a determination to win souls for the Kingdom. Pure and simple, we wanted something good to come out of this union.

Since we had already gone to Pittsburgh to knock on doors with this brother and to minister in his church without compensation, we knew he would do whatever he could to help us. We borrowed some money and traveled one way, all five of us on a plane to Pittsburgh. This brother had told us that he would make arrangements for us to live in the townhouse next to his. Yet when we got there, he had not made any such arrangements, so we ended up staying with him for approximately seven months. His wife was not saved and was not very happy about having five new people in her home without explanation. He was very controlling and it was apparent that his wife had no say in the matter.

This was another major adjustment that was imposed upon us. I tried so hard to be brave and to keep our spirits up, but sometimes it was so difficult. Henry's hands were tied, as he couldn't work. Once again, I had to take the reins and think of ways for my family and I to survive. I should have found a job and an apartment; but instead, I enrolled in the University of Pittsburgh and took some classes there. My children were enrolled in school and did pretty well in spite of the challenges they were facing. Overall, some good came out of this situation. The pastors' wife eventually received the Holy Spirit one night. We held services in the basement. However, since my husband couldn't work I perceived that his self-image was just dwindling day by day. There wasn't much that he could do about this situation. We were playing a waiting game. I received my citizenship and then we worked on getting his permanent residency.

Things were getting real tense in that home and I could see the unrest among my children. We began to look for a place of our own. When we decided to go to Pittsburgh, I told the children that we were going on a two week vacation, to see what Pittsburgh was like. Deep in our hearts, we were hoping for things to work out for us so that we could begin to grow as a family unit. We knew that the best way to build this relationship was to be involved in a thriving church.

Finally, Glory! Hallelujah! We found a place of our own and we rejoiced to see the day. We continued a relationship with this brother and gave full support to his church. It was during these times that the "Wings of Youth" after school Program was formed. Ten girls came to know the Lord through this ministry. This was purely supported by my family, especially the girls who witnessed at school, even at lunch time. I was the chauffeur on Fridays. I was a student nurse by then, and would rush from the hospital where I was training to get the girls at their school in Highland Park. My girls would have everyone all lined up to be transported to the church. What a time we would have. One after another, they came to Christ and allowed Him to make the change in their lives. We were blessed to see many of them baptized in Jesus' Name and filled with the Holy Spirit.

Even here we were faced with challenges, not just from a natural standpoint but even in the spiritual. One afternoon as we sat down to have our discussion, a man came walking into the Sanctuary and all the way to the back where we were meeting. He came up to me and asked if I could cast the demon out of him. This was a very timely occurrence. One of the girls who had just gotten saved asked me why at nights every thing came alive in her room. She had only began to notice this since she had given her life to Christ and had received the Holy Spirit.

In response, I brought their attention to II Timothy 1:7, which states, "For God has not given us the spirit of fear; but of power and of love and of a sound mind." Well, no sooner had the words came from my lips that that man walked in from off the street and came right up to me. We were using the room off the sanctuary, but the sanctuary was at street level since it was in a store-front. He came to me and asked, 'can you pray for me, I'm demon possessed'. Now I had been praying and fasting quite a bit for the spiritual growth of the group, but how was I to know the challenge I was to face that day.

Thoughts began to race through my mind. "O.K., so now I'm faced with a big one. The Pastor is not here, neither is my husband, the Assistant to the Pastor. Lord, where is Andrew (my son). He was coming over after school. Where are the men?" The only other adult was Sister Kathy, who did not belong to our local church but had a burden for young people. She was just visiting that day. Well, thank the Lord she was a prayer warrior. You should have seen the look on the girls' faces. I know in their minds they were wondering, "What is Sister Brash going to do now?" and I was praying, "Lord please help me."

Well, He did help me. For as soon as the man made his request, I tried to remember all that I had seen the men of God do back home when faced with such a challenge. Unfortunately, I hadn't seen much of this in our churches in the States. All of a sudden I heard myself giving out instructions. I commanded the man to go and kneel by the altar, and he obeyed. I asked the group to go stand on the platform and begin praying for this man. I told them not to touch him, just to pray. Then I asked the Sister who was working with me that evening to stay in the back with the new girls who had not yet received the Holy Spirit and help them to begin praying. I knew that they were experiencing great fear. We could feel it all around us.

This man looked like he was in his forties. He had pointed ears and looked evil. He also carried a book in his hand. I was seriously praying in my spirit for instruction. With everyone in place, I sought the Lord quietly to know what the next step was. I received instruction and went over to the man and asked him to say the Name Jesus. He promptly told me that he could but that it had no effect on him. He turned around and pointed to a Sunday school poster, which was on display. It was a picture of the lake of fire and I got chills when he said, "that's where I'm going." I began to pray and the girls prayed with me but to no avail.

The man had made up his mind that he was going to hell and nobody could hinder that. We prayed and cried out to God on his behalf and finally he told us that many other preachers had tried, but to no avail. He was doomed and had accepted the damnation. Since I was convinced that his mind was warped and that he was feeding his mind on the wrong thing, I felt compelled to take the book from him. He refused and I had to command him in the Name of Jesus to let go of it. He did and then it was confirmed that what he was reading was demonic. The book was about children who were demon possessed and so forth. What a horrible place to be in. He felt condemned to hell, and was walking around on earth without hope. He had obviously made his choice.

He left the sanctuary still bound. We wept for him but there was nothing that we could do. He seemed to have wanted it that way. When we returned home that night, we burned the book in Jesus Name. But something told us to expect a visitation, which was not holy. That night, it came. Andrew was working at a supermarket in the city, and would come home pretty late in the night.

On this particular night, my husband and I were awakened to the sound of footsteps. My nephew, Kareem was asleep in the front room that he shared with Andrew, my son. We must have dosed off after deciding that it was Andrew coming home. I was awakened to my husband pleading the blood and calling on the Name of Jesus. He was holding his wrist, which he stated was burning from some sort of friction. He said that there was a presence, which came into our bedroom and proceeded to cut his wrist. It did not succeed as it was intercepted by another Presence, which was greater. It certainly didn't leave the same way it came in. Glory to God!

As a family, we worked with this Ministry for a little while longer, and the Lord was with us. We learned quite a bit about success and failures, triumphs and defeats. We lost a few battles but knew that by faith we would eventually win the war. The fact that we came through each challenge and still had each other was enough to encourage me to go on. We endeavored to always look at the bright side of things and to say that it must be the will of the Lord for us to keep going. He was fashioning us for a greater ministry. We didn't stay down too long. The one thing we certainly had in common was music and singing. We sang a lot at home. That was one sure way of encouraging ourselves in the Lord.

We joined another Ministry in town and that was a major transition for us. The Pastor and church family were very warm to us and welcomed us. Soon we were becoming involved in one way or another. My children began to make new friends and to settle in. They were asked to join the choir and even had lead parts at times. I can still remember the first time Charmaine sang a lead in one of the concerts. I was still a little shy about singing in this church, since it seemed like everybody could sing so well. But Miss Char was bold and just got up there and sang. We were elated and so proud of her. Well, we just thank and praise the Lord for all His blessings. He gives gifts and they do make room for those who possess them.

We spent four good years in Pittsburgh and eventually returned to New York. Charmaine married in August 1988 and it was quite beautiful to see her being walked down the aisle by her step father Henry. It was another milestone in our lives. Although I was not quite ready to let her go, she bonded with a young man who compliments her in the music ministry.

We settled in Springfield Gardens New York and continued our ministry of music at the church in Queens, New York. We saw tremendous growth while in that church, and the music ministry played a great part in the growth process. We put on concerts and sang in various other churches. Everything was to the glory of God. It was shortly after we had become involved with the music ministry at this church, that a brother from Jamaica mentioned another ministry opportunity in North Chicago, Illinois. At the time, we just sort of dismissed this suggestion and went on with our lives. We were on a journey with so many bumps in the road.

In October of that year, I had a gall bladder attack and was forced to have it removed. I was desperately ill and spent three weeks in the La Guardia hospital. After the surgery, my bilirubin was quite unstable and I was diagnosed with Hepatitis A. I became quite jaundiced and had lost so much weight that my head seemed bigger than my body.

When I was released from the hospital, it was with tubes in my side. I was quite distraught. At the time, I had a temporary job and did not qualify for sick time or sick pay. Andrew and Michelle were living at home and they were able to assist Henry with the finances. This was a very trying time for all of us.

Even in this, God stepped in to give me a spiritual awakening. I remember one day being home by myself and feeling really depressed, when something happened to motivate me to pray. I started praying and felt that I was being prompted to call a particular telephone number. When I eventually made contact with someone at that number, I found out that the person I called was a 30-year-old young woman who was suicidal. She had lost her mother around Christmas time some years before. It was quite a traumatic experience for her and every year around that time she would attempt to take her life.

I spoke with her for about an hour and was able to minister to her. I was even privileged to take her to church with me. Needless to say, I wasn't quite sure what the Lord was doing with my life. It just did not make sense to me. What was the purpose of this experience? I have since lost contact with her, but I pray that the seed planted in her life will germinate and that someday we will meet again.

Shortly before the gallbladder attack I had committed to sing with the mass choir of our District in an upcoming concert. I did not allow the tubes in my side to stop me. As soon as I could, I attended rehearsal and decided that I would lead this choir in the song "He touched me," if it was the last thing I did. When the night of the concert came, I still had tubes in my side, but I sang with everything I could muster and the Lord anointed me to sing. Souls were blessed that night, proving that God can keep you and will use you if you avail yourself, even in the midst of afflictions.

God was not through with us yet, and was getting ready to show Himself in a super natural way in our lives again. He had another miracle for us. Oh thank you Jesus! It was in October 1990 when Charmaine and her baby daughter Veronica had come to visit us in New York. On this particular evening her husband decided that he would meet us half way to collect his family. We delivered them safely; and since my husband was tired, I decided that I would drive home. I started traveling across the George Washington Bridge and came to a point in the road where there were construction vehicles parked on the right side. I drove in the far left lane to avoid them. All of a sudden, a young woman, who was obviously drunk (liquor was found in the trunk of her car), came speeding up on the right side of us. As quickly as I saw her headlights flash in the right-side view mirror of the car, I heard what sounded like a click and the car went out of control.

It was as if someone with a giant hand had picked up the car and was bouncing it against the wall, which divided the bridge. It felt like a battle being waged as all four tires of the car were bounced on the wall at the same time. As inertia took over, I let go of the steering wheel and my feet were shaken off the pedals. There was nothing left for me to do but wait it out in prayer. Henry, who had been dozing just prior to the incident, moved into action and I heard him cry, "JESUS. " Immediately, the bouncing stopped and the car settled. But the negotiation was not over. That other power was determined to destroy us that night, and began to bounce the car again. This time it seemed like it was going to go over the other side of the divider. This would have caused us to fall in the midst of oncoming traffic. One can only imagine what the outcome could have been, but God said," NOT SO!".

I felt like the angels of God came down and took control of the situation, as once more, my husband cried out, "JESUS."

The car settled down peacefully as it did before and bounced across the road to the opposite side away from the oncoming traffic and rested safely. Although we were a little bit dazed, our first instinct was to check to see if either of us was hurt. We began to praise the Lord for sparing our lives. To top it off, the tape player in the car was still going and the choir began to sing, "Thank You Lord for Another Day."

I immediately got out of the car to check on the people in the car that had hit us. The two young ladies suffered serious injuries. It didn't appear that they were wearing their seat belts. One suffered a fractured skull and the other lost some teeth when her mouth hit the dashboard. Blood was everywhere.

I stayed with the young ladies until the paramedics and the police came. I then took a good look at the entire scene before me. There seemed to be people everywhere. What caught my attention was that on this four-lane highway, the traffic had stopped and was being blocked by several big trucks that were behind us. And then it dawned on me that we were the cause for this hullabaloo. Oh, how true are the words to the song:

Oh, sweet wonder,
Oh sweet wonder
Jesus the Son of God
Oh how I love Him
How I adore Him
Jesus, the Son of God

He's my deliverer
He's my deliverer

Jesus, the Son of God
And oh, how I love Him
How I adore Him
Jesus, the Son of God!

As soon as we could assure the paramedics that we were fine and had given all of our necessary information to the police, we decided that it was time to leave. We were so scared that we were going to be in more trouble since our insurance had expired and we had not had a chance to renew it. We were in transition and these events began to take place one after the other – we had no breathing room.

Since we had no visible serious injuries and didn't know the scale of the damage done to the car, we decided that we would continue to drive home and deal with all the rest in the morning. We continued on our journey, with me at the steering wheel again.

Suddenly, the tires gave way and I realized that we were driving on the rims. Henry told me to pull over. Fortunately, we had just reached a safe place where we could park the car and plan our next move. Keep in mind this was New York City and the corner was cold and dark. We didn't have cell phones back then and there were no pay phones in sight. We just did what we knew how to do, we began to pray and the more we prayed the braver we became.

The next thing I knew, we were both standing outside of our car and were waving like crazy at the passing motorists. We were on the Cross Island Parkway. When it seemed like no one was brave enough to stop, a Mercedes Benz pulled up in front of us. The driver of the car was a Jamaican recording artist. He showed up, cell phone and all, and after he listened to our story, he invited us to sit in his car and make any necessary telephone calls. We called one of the brothers from the church and without hesitation; he and his wife came to our rescue. This gentleman waited with us until the brother and his wife showed up. They brought a thermos of hot mint tea and then took us home and out of the cold. We knew then that the Lord had not abandoned us.

God showed us that He was with us, even in those circumstances. Isn't that just like God!

We had so much to thank God for in this event. Not only did He protect us from serious bodily injuries, but also warded off the accident until my daughter and baby were safely out of the car. On the way to meet her husband, she did not even have her seat belt on and the baby was not secured in a car seat. Great is Thy faithfulness! Even in our folly, He is looking out for us. I am grateful to Him for allowing us to go through these challenges to His glory. He did not leave us but stayed with us, even to the end. We were finally home and that was what really mattered. We didn't have the money to fix the car right away and drove it shamelessly wherever we went. No doubt, there were those who laughed at us or pitied us. We found out the next day that we both had suffered cervical injuries and whiplash. That was alright, we didn't let it phase us, we just kept right on going. Thank you Jesus!

We thought that we would be given a little reprieve, but there were more trials to come. You can imagine how excited we were when we received the settlement from the accident. We immediately began to search for a car. Oh Glory, Hallelujah, soon we will be like normal people, driving a normal vehicle. We checked the papers and found an advertisement about a 1982 Maxima, and what caught our eyes was that the price was right and it was fully loaded.

With newspaper in hand we started on our journey. We were as excited as two small children on Christmas morning as we searched for the address where we would find this car. After we examined the vehicle, we became very excited about owning a car such as this. Although it was an older model, it was attractive and had a system which even talked. It would tell us if we were low on gas or if lights were on, plus many other features. We were able to purchase it for $3,000.

As was the case for most people living in our area in Springfield Gardens, we had to park on the street. A parking place was definitely a premium and sometimes people became very irate if someone parked in their selected spot. Henry mentioned to me that he noticed tampering of the car door one morning. He didn't think too much about it until the next morning when he went outside to go to work and found the car missing from where he had parked it. Although the police came and made a report, they were never able to find the vehicle. We just wrote it off as loss.

We needed a car to get to work, school and church since public transportation was not available to take us to all these places conveniently, so we rented another vehicle soon after with the help of a friend. Within a week or so, it too was stolen. The robbers had a sense of humor for they took the new white Dynasty and left us an old beat up light blue Dynasty with the motor running (possibly through the night) and ignition wires hanging out. Just imagine how we felt! Why were these things happening to us? Oh, Lord, not again. When would it end?

Let me hasten to assure you that with every challenge, there was a victory. Sometime around November 1989, there was a big tornado in New York City. The news flash stated that there were about five tornadoes, which traveled over the connecting bridges between New York City and New Jersey. This was unprecedented and really did some damage as they moved across the land. In Springfield Gardens we experienced heavier than normal rain showers with thunder and lightning. We must have eventually fallen asleep when all of a sudden I heard what sounded like a crack.

I opened my eyes, simultaneously with my husband as a flash of lightening came through our window towards where I was laying. He was having a vision that involved him in a negotiation for my life. Henry made the right choice and the Lord led him to cover me from the evil of the night. I awoke in time to hear him plead the blood of Jesus while– his arm was stretched out over me! On the news the next day, there were stories of people being killed by lightening during that violent storm. Once again, the Lord protected me.

All of these events certainly caused us to start thinking about making a change. But what kind of change would it be? Well, we found out soon enough. Henry began to share his vision for ministry with me. We were fulfilling one aspect and did not have a clue how the other three parts would be realized. We began to earnestly seek the Lord. We prayed about our involvement in the church that we were attending and we prayed about the "prophecies" or "words of wisdom" or "words of knowledge" that were spoken to us from time to time.

We were desperate for direction, because something had to change. Things were getting rather intense. Then we remembered the ministry opportunity in Illinois. The church was in transition and needed a pastor. To my knowledge, my husband had not shared with this brother that he had a pastoral calling. However, this brother knew that Henry had received formal training at the Caribbean Bible Institute in Jamaica. He gave us a few more details about the church and suggested that we consider visiting them.

He told us that this group of people (mostly family members) had left a United Pentecostal Church in the area and were now building a church of their own. They were going through a legal battle with the present pastor, and to his knowledge, they were looking for someone to fill the role of a pastor quite soon. The whole thing sounded so complicated, we decided not to give it another thought.

One Friday my husband and I came home from work and were in a thoughtful mood when a telephone call came from a lady whom we had never met and had never talked to before. After she identified herself and told us where she was from, we figured it out. She was from the church in Illinois. We accepted her invitation to visit them for a weekend. When we arrived, we ministered on Friday night and all day Sunday. They were very gracious, and we returned to New York with a great burden, especially for the precious children we met there.

My cry to the Lord was, "Why? Why do the children have to go through all this pain?" As they shared some of what had taken place, I wondered why the perpetrators were still alive. I did not know that such things could occur in church and between so called "brethren." Why weren't the guilty struck down? They broke so many of God's commandments. They caused havoc in the church. Then I remembered "His merciful kindness is great towards us and His truth endures to all generations."

When we returned to New York, we tried to continue with life as usual but it wasn't easy. We finally made up our minds that we were going back to Illinois. There was no explanation, but we had to go back. When we presented our decision to our Pastor and his assistant, we could tell that they did not understand. We felt compelled to go to the next level. We were actually going to boot camp and didn't know it.

The announcement was made that "the Brashes were leaving New York City" and it began to spread all over the region. A wonderful celebration was held in our honor. After we received all of the cards, gifts, and words of encouragement, we were on our own. We had a great send off from the folks at our church. There was one couple that went out of their way to encourage us and wish us well. They did this right up until the night we drove away. We thank the Lord for them! Acts 13:3, "And when they had fasted and prayed, and laid their hands on them, they sent them away."

Finally, everything was settled, Andrew, Michelle and our new granddaughter, Victoria would move over to Brooklyn and share an apartment. I couldn't believe that I was leaving my Tori in New York, she was the granddaughter I was helping to raise. But we were on a mission. We left them our furniture and packed the few belongings we decided to take with us in the truck. We hugged those who had come to pray for us and to see us off. We got in a truck we rented from Ryder and said "good bye" to New York City one more time, right in the dead of winter.

We were so exhausted we had to spend the night in New Jersey. We just did not feel like rushing the trip. It was still snowing and my husband was not used to driving the moving truck yet. We felt like we were going to meet our destiny and nothing could hinder us now, not even winter! Since Pittsburgh was about halfway to Illinois, we decided to stop there and spend a night with Charmaine and her family.

The trip over the mountains and around the winding roads was a great challenge because of the snow. Imagine driving a truck that you were not accustomed to in this kind of weather. Sometimes we could not see the road because of zero visibility. We then discovered that the truck had a leak. What a sight it must have been to see me stuffing tissue paper along the windows trying to prevent the water from coming in. We were in deep intercession for our warmth and protection. At times I doubted if we were going to make it. But we kept going. We thought about how the Apostle Paul had fulfilled his purpose and it brought us strength.

I remember a time during that trip when we were almost in a head on collision with a 18 wheeler oil truck. We were very grateful when we reached Altoona, PA and breathed a prayer of thankfulness when we saw the exit signs to Pittsburgh. The Lord had been very gracious to us. We continued to trust Him to keep us safe for the remainder of the journey.

We felt like we were on a missionary journey. Thankfully, we were not walking over mountainous terrains carrying such heavy backpacks, that if we leaned too far back, we could fall to our death. At least, we were driving in a vehicle, leak and all. Our prayer was, "We will follow wherever you lead." Our hearts pulsated with anticipation and expectation. We had no clue how this whole thing was going to turn out. We only knew that if Jesus had anything to do with it, it would turn out all right and for our good.

New York City brought us much heartache and we just wanted to get away. We would only return to minister someday on an evangelistic campaign. We were able to rest in Pittsburgh before tackling the remainder of the trip. We spent a while in prayer asking God to make the rest of the trip less challenging. It was so good to spend the night with family. The babies were growing so beautifully. I didn't even feel like a grandmother, but here I was, almost 42 years old and already a grandmother of three.

We finally headed to the Midwest. I did feel like we were pioneers without the horse and buggy. I remembered the eyes of the little children in that church and I could hear their voices singing beautiful songs that I would soon teach them. I began to dream about how this church would turn around and become the ideal example of wholesomeness, regardless of all the legal battles and ungodly acts. I had confidence that my husband would turn out to be the one they were looking for. It was a great vision! Surely, this must be what the

Lord was telling me in that scripture, Micah 4:10 Yes, we have left the City, New York City, and now, we are on our way to the "Field."

In this "Field," we should find some treasures and we shall be delivered from the hand of our enemies. The rest of the journey turned out to be a cake walk as we drove through Ohio. I believe they have the rental trucks rigged so they can't go over the speed limit. We were crossing through States and loving it. There is no feeling like the feeling of doing the perfect will of God. It causes a person to sing with gusto and fervency. There is an abounding confidence that just engulfs the soul who is blessed with such a revelation.

Boot Camp

We came in to Illinois, in February 1992, bursting with desire to plunge into our new role as Pastor and Pastor's wife. Oh my, the challenges were waiting. Boot camp was only a breath away and our training had just begun! There was an apartment already prepared for us and this time it was as promised, so that went well. We knew where to go, who to contact, and they were available for us. We got settled and spent the next few days opening the gifts and cards that were showered on us at the going away celebration. We marveled that so many cared about our well being. Most of the folks who contributed were from our home church back in Jamaica. Such wondrous love was shown! I want to again say, THANK YOU, to those who helped to launch us on this missions journey.

My husband started his duties right away. There was a brother who was a deacon of the church and he saw to it that Henry was busy. He called very early in the mornings. He worked nights at a nursing home and on his way home from work, he just supposed that the pastor should be up at that time of the morning. Obviously, he didn't consider the possibility of the pastor being up and praying at four o'clock in the morning and was trying to rest awhile after prayer. Needless to say, we did not look forward to those telephone calls!

I immediately moved into action with my husband and reinforced a good prayer foundation. He and I would pray together at noon everyday when we were home. We would also meet with a small group once a week at the church. Then there was mid-week prayer, Bible Study and a Youth Night. We were also meeting at the church twice on Sundays. We were determined to develop a church filled with Bible believing saints. For a little while it seemed like things were going perfectly. We were sending good reports to those in New York, my mother included. She remained quite skeptical about the whole thing.

The youth and adult choirs made great contribution to the services. We were told that the music in the church had never sounded better. However, we could sense that there were lingering concerns. Since this was the first time we functioned in a pastoral role, we were unsure of the appropriate responses toward certain behaviors. We did have an overseer and his decision could override that of the local minister.

Before long we were able to identify a small group of people who were committed to resisting our efforts at the church. We found out that their resistance was due to each of them being passed over for the positions we now held. We found ourselves at times in the middle of the two opposing factions in the church. Everybody had a story, and after all the bickering I would have such bad headaches I didn't think that I would make it in the next day.

Nevertheless, God kept us. Even though my husband was compensated by the church, I went back to work in April, and soon we were able to purchase a car of our own. My husband had been using the church van for a few months and on many occasions there was no heat in it. We did not complain, we were thankful to be able to serve others. And serve we did. He would even opt to be the driver when we would go to visit other churches. He didn't expect to be served, but would always seek to be the servant.

Our desire to see the church grow motivated us to seek ways to let others know about the ministry there. We would even take the youth choir out to sing in the mall and at nursing homes in the area. This was a great experience, especially for the children. They really enjoyed those events! We worked hard to keep the spirits of the people high and encouraged them to stay focused on the Lord's work. We tried to involve everyone in every program.

We were just about halfway through the year and though everything appeared to be going well, things began to decline. The division in the church became even more obvious. The scripture states that a house divided against itself will not stand. It broke my heart when I realized that we were dealing with a lot of hypocrisy. Before long the whole church body was negatively affected.

Proverbs 4:7 states, "Wisdom is the principal thing; therefore get wisdom: and with all thy getting get understanding." This has become one of my dearest instructional scriptures, as I have learned that God has all kinds of children and only He knows what they are capable of doing. Henry would preach messages that were more like a plea for the ones sowing discord to change their ways and consider how they dealt with their brothers and sisters in Christ. He would encourage the congregation to love and forgive one another. While he preached, I would intercede. We were the dynamic duo in the spirit.

We began to feel a change and there was nothing we could do about it. I felt a spirit of discouragement taking hold of me. It was like a cloak of darkness had come over us and was trying to snuff out our light. There was division in the church. The saints were discussing whether or not "we" should stay longer than a year or leave once our time was served. One of their major concerns was that my husband wanted to apply for his license with the United Pentecostal Church and they did not want that. One lady told us after a meeting, wherever we went, she would follow. But the negative attitudes were also very evident. I'm convinced that a person's basic nature remains the same even after they come in contact with Jesus. Victory over the flesh only comes through a daily surrendering of self.

One Sunday evening, I sat in the service feeling quite uncomfortable. We were told that our contract was not to be renewed, but that we were welcome to continue attending the church to provide the music. Right then I sought the Lord and He answered in His word. He led me to Acts 18:9 and 10, "Be not afraid, but speak, and hold not thy peace; for I am with thee, and no man shall set on thee to hurt thee, for I have much people in this City." I immediately felt a surge of courage in my spirit, and I was ready for whatever would come next. We could have used some fellowship right about then.

We finished out the year right up to the first day of 1993. I led the church in a "victory" march. After church I ate breakfast which was prepared by some of the church members. I became very ill, with excruciating pains in my lower abdomen, and had to be rushed to Victory Hospital later in the day. They could not tell us what caused it. I felt like Satan was mocking us, but I knew the Lord had everything in control. I could not believe in this day of high technology and advanced medicine; the doctor ordered good old-fashioned castor oil. I came home after a few days and recuperated quickly. We left with mixed emotions. I am still amazed that human beings can be so wrong and still think that they are right. So many times the Lord tries to get our attention long enough to impart his desires for us but we just keep resisting Him. After a while, He just steps back and allows us to continue until we hit a brick wall. He is such a loving Father who will not turn away from us when we cry out to Him for help. He will run to us in our moment of need. I love Him so much!

There were times when I was so immensely blessed by the powerful anointed ministry of my husband, but I couldn't help but notice the dry critical eyes staring back at him. I'm sure this is very hard for any Pastor's wife and children. Only God can keep us through those hard times.

Chapter 9

Zion, Beautiful Zion!

...that I may shew forth all thy praise in the gates of the daughter of Zion: I will rejoice in thy salvation-Psalm 9:1(KJV)

We began to pray again together to find the mind of God. Where to from here Lord? Zion was revealed to us. So we prayed some more for direction how to proceed, and God gave it to us. Why Zion? I did not have the answer and neither did Henry. Yet, somehow we were drawn to this little city. It sits approximately nine square miles north of Waukegan, Illinois and at the time of my writing this book, had approximately 22,000 residents.

The city was built by Dr. John Alexander Dowie, a minister from Australia, in the early 1900s. It was built to keep in the good and keep out the bad. To live within the city limits one had to be committed to keeping all the laws that were set forth. Drugs, alcohol, tobacco, movie theaters, dance halls and houses of ill repute were all barred. It was meant to be a replica of the 'Holy Jerusalem'. All the streets were named after Bible characters or places mentioned in the Bible.

Dr. Dowie had a congregation of thousands. And they were quite loyal to him. His dream and vision was to build many cities like "Zion" all over the world. His healing ministry was the highlight and he became quite known for his disapproval of medical doctors and their practices. Many powerful Holy Ghost revivals were conducted in the city and it is recorded that in 1906, over 500 ministers of the gospel received the baptism of the Holy Ghost there. When we canvass the area we have had the pleasure of meeting descendents of Dr. Dowie's original congregation.

Without even knowing the history of Zion, On February 14, 1993, we started "The Endtime Apostolic Tabernacle" ministry at the Leisure Center in Zion, Illinois. What a day of rejoicing! We had twenty-seven in attendance. We started with Sunday school and the presence of the Lord was always in the place. People began to receive the Holy Ghost, even children. The group grew quickly. We needed a place of our own as we were getting tired of moving our equipment back and forth every Sunday. We prayed and God led us to a building on Sheridan Road. This building was located in an unincorporated area. It was between Zion and Winthrop Harbor. The owner of the building served on the County Board.

We had church there for three years. Our District Superintendent, Home Missions Director, and other preachers came and preached for us there.

The building sat between a roller rink and bowling alley. On Sunday nights, the roller rink would be jam packed with young people mostly from Wisconsin and Chicago. The Lord protected us so many times from danger. I remember trying to get out of church and being blocked in by the cars that would be parked right up against the building. The owner, when notified, would call in the assistance of the police department and they would come to direct the traffic for us to get out safely.

We grew tired of the distractions and began to pray that God would deliver us and shut down the Sunday Night interference. Especially after one young man challenged me when I told him that this was a church and that they were inconveniencing us. We also became pro-active and put tracts on the cars, after that they never bothered us again. God stopped it right there, praise His Name forever. That was another victory. To God be the glory! I wish we had the manpower to reach those young people. We could have experienced a great revival in this.

Church services were great; people were getting the Holy Ghost. We knocked down walls and spread out to the other side of the building. The ministerial staff grew. People were coming to every service in full force. There was one particular Pastor who would bring his entire church every time that he would visit. He had a group of fired up young people who would impact our young people in a positive way. We had youth revivals and campfires in the church yard where we would roast marshmallows, hot dogs and corn.

The youth would look forward to these events with great anticipation, as the big white church bus would come rolling in, jam-packed with eager faces ready to "rumble" for Jesus. They were ready for their deliverance and invariably would receive it. I remember a co-worker of mine, a former High School Principal from New England and Catholic by religion, coming to one of these events and he just stood in amazement at what he saw. His comment was, "I believe I have finally found the way." My prayer is that he never stops until he is fully on the right path.

It was during one of those fiery hot Sunday night youth revivals, that we noticed someone looking through the window. We recognized the young man's face, so one of our brothers went out to invite him in, but he declined. We were sure God still had it all arranged. The following Tuesday morning, Henry was in the church office preparing for our Prayer and Bible Study. He felt like the Lord was prompting him to get the mail. That's what he thought, until he came face to face with the young man at the empty mailbox. God was actually saying- GO GET THE MALE!

It was the same young man who was looking through the window on Sunday Night. He proceeded to tell Henry that he was on his way home from the bar that night, but something drew his attention to the building. His curiosity heightened when he looked in and saw all those young people. They were of varied ethnic backgrounds and looked so happy. What an open door! Without hesitation, Henry proceeded to tell him about the service at 7:30 p.m. The young man did not hesitate. This was what he had been searching for, and he promptly went home to the trailer park across the street, to get ready for church. He came in that night with his Bible in hand beaming with a hunger and thirst for righteousness.

He started to attend church faithfully and at one time he also lived with us. It was such a joy for us to open our home to a new convert. He began to pray, fast and read the Word. One Sunday after a Sunday School lesson from the book of Acts, about the Day of Pentecost; he went to the altar and received the Holy Ghost, speaking in tongues as the Spirit gave him the utterance. He was baptized that same day in the precious Name of Jesus and we rejoiced since he was actually our first "walk-in" new convert.

Things were going so well, until one evening he had a visitor at the church that was a former acquaintance of his. This young man came in and discouraged him from serving the Lord. He was not strong enough and gave heed to his old ways. We pray that one day he will return to the Lord and serve Him only!

People were being healed and delivered in every service. In one of these services a mom and her three pre-teen children got saved. She also had a baby. The mother began to have heart problems and was taken to Brigham Womens' Hospital in Boston, Massachusetts. The diagnosis was an enlarged heart. When we heard that they wanted to do a heart transplant, the other prayer warriors and I decided this was a drastic situation which called for drastic measures.

One of the other Sisters in the church and I flew to Boston to lay hands on her. We fasted and prayed all the way. When we arrived, we visited another Apostolic Church in the area and received confirmation that the Lord had already healed her. She later testified that after we prayed and left, she was taken to the operating room for the surgery. As they prepped her for surgery, the new heart that was deemed a good match began to roll all over the table and they decided they could not proceed. She was taken back to her room and released a few days after with just a few words of caution from her doctor. The doctor told her that there was no need for surgery to be performed. The church praised and magnified the Lord for He had done marvelous things. One more time, He performed a miracle.

The spirit of discontentment and criticism crept into the church and found a few accommodating souls. We recognized this familiar spirit and knew it couldn't be allowed to run its course. This could spread like a virus and will destroy an organization or any institution, even a church. In Ecclesiastes 10:1, the Bible declares that, "Dead flies cause the ointment of the apothecary to send forth a stinking savor: so doth a little folly him that is in reputation for wisdom and honor."

Right up until mid 1995, things were moving quite harmoniously. I remember a Brother and his wife brought their tent all the way from Booneville, Mississippi, so we could have a Tent Crusade. It was one of the most awesome experiences that we ever had. Folks received the Holy Ghost and were delivered. God is a miracle worker, and He will never be indebted to anyone.

We began to feel resistance to the ministry once we started planning this event. But we went forward none the less. Money was scarce, but the Lord did provide. As the Brother was setting up the tent, a gentleman came up to him and gave him $150.00. He simply said, "God told me to give this to you". He then proceeded to ask for the pastor, who was inside the building. He promptly went in and took out $400.00 and handed it to my husband. He told him that it was God's money and that he was instructed to give it to him and he was obedient. There were awesome signs and wonders at that crusade. Praise the Lord from whom all blessings flow!

It was quite amazing to me that even in the midst of the flow of the Holy Ghost, there were some who became downright rebellious. There were ethnic struggles. We had never experienced this before and really tried our best to resolve these conflicts, but to no avail. One lady was quite disrespectful to my husband on more than one occasion. She was also manipulative, and although I recognized it, I could do nothing about it except cry out to God.

If I knew then what I know now, things would probably have turned out quite differently. Ministry requires one to be 'dead' to themselves. You don't exist anymore. I think of Moses and all that he went through. It didn't seem fair when the people he risked his life for turned against him, disrespected and disregarded the sacrifices he made on their behalf. I read the biblical account and I empathize with him and his wife. I consider them the first ones to pastor a church. Sometimes I wish there was more written about Zipporah in the Bible. I would like to know how she supported her husband when he became frustrated and began to question his call to the ministry. His father-in-law had to step in and give him wise counsel about his responsibilities, including his wife. Exodus 18:13-23 describes the full account.

I encouraged my husband to not become weary in the work of the ministry. As soon as I sensed that he was becoming mentally drained or challenged, I would formulate a plan to bring him back to normalcy. I would do this balancing or juggling act continuously and I was consumed by it. I found myself totally caught up in service to everyone else. Are there ever any clear answers? Since I had encouraged him to start this work in Zion, I really didn't want to see him fail. I felt that this was what the Lord wanted us to do. We didn't leave New York to come to Illinois to fail. I am convinced that true leaders are made by trial and error especially when dealing with people of varied backgrounds. It takes time and consistent training to learn the techniques of conflict resolution.

Financially, we weren't doing too badly. Almost everyone who worked paid tithes and gave offerings, including me. Henry was full-time and the people did not mind, as long as their needs were met. We enjoyed our fellowship with local ministers. I was always delighted to see him interact with other pastors. They need encouragement and mentoring from one another, but I always had such a burden for the pastors' wives.

Sometimes they are so neglected. Some, like myself, go into this ministry with the wrong concept. One can become so caught up in the romanticism of it. However, you soon find out that it is really hard work. I still consider it a great honor to be called into this service beside my husband.

We had more lessons to learn. We found ourselves with a pretty good sized youth group but no chosen leader. We were somewhat overwhelmed just dealing with the adults. I had what I thought was a good idea. Let's bring my son in to fulfill this role. After all, he knew our worship. I couldn't think of a better fit. Surely, he would comply and work within the parameters already in place. Oh, I had it all worked out. I had a vision of a fired up youth group, being involved in youth events such as Bible quizzing and youth camps.

Imagine my consternation when my husband objected. He thought it was an unwise decision, but he didn't deliberate. He obviously should have. I'm sure, it would have sunken in at some point or another that there were young men under our ministry who were capable of functioning in this capacity. I wish he had put his foot down. Oh God, please bless our pastors and wives to be sensitive to your voice always, to know when to stand still and when to go forward!

At this time, we were training people to fill leadership roles in the developing departments. However, there was some hesitation in turning over the youth department into their hands. We needed a youth leader who would be communicative and dependable. He or she should also show due respect to their leaders and fulfill their roles within the boundaries of the assembly. We felt that we had just cause for concern, as we had been faced with some resistance to our leadership on occasion.

So, I began to think about a possible solution to this whole thing.

I finally convinced my husband to bring on our son as youth minister. It appeared that the church board and members were all supportive of the decision. Then one of the ministers immediately decided that he was not coming back to our church because he thought we didn't like him anymore. In his mind we were bringing our son in to take his place. Some found other ways to show their disapproval. Oh, it was a big mess. We tried with everything in our powers to bring order but it only became worse.

The fires of doubt and dismay began to burn. In a short while even the relationship between my son and I was strained. The waves of destruction began to sweep over the church body and all kinds of strange events began to take place. As someone so rightly said, the enemy came but for one purpose, to conquer and divide. He is a thief who comes only to steal, kill and destroy, if we let him. This could have been dubbed, 'the darkest year of my life'. But, no, there was more to come. While we were going through the challenges, we were being changed, formed and fashioned to come out victoriously. Many times we sought the help of intercessors and mentors but found none. Now I look back and am convinced that the Lord wanted to fill those roles Himself.

You can imagine just how torn up I was. How could such a plan not work? How can folks who seemingly believe the 'same' thing, end up on opposite sides, and so quickly? The church on a whole was experiencing clashes in the house and when we tried to settle these issues, well, folks withdrew themselves from my husband and I and sought refuge elsewhere. Henry was beginning to be openly challenged by some. They began to look at us differently.

Inappropriate actions should not be ignored in any ministry. The devil is quite cunning and is always seeking to bring the man or woman of God to a weak and ineffective state. One church member would bypass the offering plate; and place her offering in my husband's coat pocket. The words of my District Superintendent in New York rang out loud and clear to me. Beware of such familiarities. There might be an ulterior motive. That was a word to the wise.

It would save a lot of heartaches, if adults would be wiser in discussing church affairs around children. How unwise we all are at times. Because adults were constantly discussing church affairs in the presence of children, it was inevitable, the children became contaminated and began to show really bad attitudes. Church became a mockery to them. They were not praying anymore. They only showed defiance, you could see it on their faces. Today, some are still out of fellowship with Christ. They refuse to come to the house of God and make a commitment. Some even dare to come into the building but they do not enter into His presence anymore. The cry of my heart is to see these young people who are now mostly adults get back to the altar, surrendering their lives to the King of Kings and Lord of Lords and then continue to walk the walk and talk the talk.

I decided to start a Christian School in this building. I had the needs of the children of the church at heart and wanted to reach out to the community. I was inspired by the Marva Collins story. So I went back to school to get a degree in Christian Education. I enrolled in an accelerated course and received my master of Christian Education degree. I was trying to do so much with so little that the pressure was too much for me. I didn't know it then, but I was becoming really sick.

Tolosa-Hunt

In February 1996 I went to work as usual, but began to experience the most excruciating pain on the right side of my face. I thought it was my sinuses, but an MRI revealed inflammation in the Oculomotor nerve. This caused swelling in my right eye. The eyeball was pulled from its normal location and lodged over into the upper right corner of the socket. Ptosis set in and the eyelid just sort of flopped down.

This was really scary. I had lost so much weight only to put on about three times more when I was put on Prednisone, the anti-inflammatory agent of choice to bring the swelling down. What an experience that was. My eye stayed like that for ten weeks and all through that time I just kept right on going to church and praying for my deliverance. The disease was called Tolosa-Hunt Syndrome. I had never heard of it before and only a few doctors were familiar with it.

This disease fell in the category of 'a rare disorder'. It came with nausea and vomiting at times. Since my eye became light sensitive, in order to go outside of the home, I had to wear an eye patch for protection. I would go to mid-day prayer at the church and as the saints prayed for me I began to experience my healing from the Lord.

I could not work although I tried briefly. My husband also had no secular job so we were basically functioning on unemployment and whatever housing allowance he received from the church. At the end of the year we found out that we had actually lived on a little over $9,000 income. The rent for our apartment was approximately $700 and the church rent was $900.00. My God is an awesome God and He's still in the miracle working business. There is no limit to His abundance.

This was the time to trust God. Our faith was being tested and many times my prayer was, 'Lord don't let me fail'. Well, He didn't let me down. The cost for the MRI was $2,000. Then there were doctor's visits and the cost for prescriptions and so forth. Where would all this money come from to pay all these expenses? Only God knew. That year we were even blessed with an offering of $500 from Mother's Memorial in our organization. We were featured in the Ladies magazine 'Reflections' as recipients of such assistance.

I could hardly comb my hair since my head was so tender. My face had become so swollen, my features changed. Amazingly, Henry thought I was quite 'cute'. To tell the truth, it didn't bother me at the time what people thought. Strange as it might seem, I felt like I was just hidden inside this body. I know we really are. But, it was like I had just put on this new costume or something and since it wasn't permanent, well, I'll just wear it until...

The medication changed my personality. I don't think that I was particularly mean or anything and it amazed me how well adjusted the folks were at the church. The children would even joke with me about my eye patch.

One little guy jokingly requested that I lend it to him so he could take it to school for show and tell. How cute! Anyway, no one made me feel out of place.

I forgot to mention the effect of this change on my family. My husband was quite unnerved and apprehensive. He'd seen me sick before, but this, this was something unfamiliar. Not even the doctors understood its origin and they certainly didn't have the cure. So, when the girls heard what happened they immediately came from Pittsburgh with the grandchildren to see about me. God bless them. They came in and surprised me.

I was so very happy to see them, but I wasn't thrilled that they saw me looking so broken. I had always tried to put my best foot forward. But this time, I was too broken to even try to find a 'best foot'. Something was going on here that was too sinister for pretense. They cried and I cried with them the best I could. Prednisone had sort of masked my feelings. My diet was changed and so forth. I had become so sensitive. Still we all held on to each other. In moments of crisis you will find out who's really for you and who's against you.

Things began to level off and by the time the girls left, well; it didn't seem quite as bad. We coped the best we could, my husband waiting on me hand and foot. In April of that year we were even able to go to San Antonio to the Home Missions Conference. By this time, my face had started to come down a bit since I was tapering off the drug. My skin had changed so I didn't even look quite the way I used to. There were blotches on my skin and I tried not to be too self-conscious about it.

Have you ever heard the saying, 'when the going gets tough, the tough gets going!,' well, that was me. Not only did I not stay home from church, I was teaching Sunday School, singing, assisting my husband in church related matters as usual. You know what, the devil didn't quit and neither did I.

My dear husband, here he was trying to keep this ship afloat and then wham- his wife and right hand person gets knocked down. But you know what the scripture says in II Corinthians 4:8-9- "we are troubled on every side, yet not distressed, we are perplexed but not in despair; persecuted but not forsaken; cast down but not destroyed." I still got up and did what I had to do.

Every now and then the Lord would send me a word of reassurance. I remember when we celebrated the church's third anniversary and this brother gave me a word from the Lord. It was taken from Isaiah 41:10, "Fear thou not; for I am with thee: be not dismayed; for I am thy God: I will strengthen thee; yea, I will help thee; yea, I will uphold thee with the right hand of my righteousness." Whew, I shouted that night especially when I sang "The Healer's in the house". I felt God's healing power surge through me like lightening. Too bad we can't stay in that presence all the time. All too soon, we were back to reality and we didn't like what we saw.

Back to reality

We began to feel added pressure. The saints were disgruntled and complaining. It seemed my husband's messages were always coming forth as warnings. There was sin in the camp. I was so weak and tired that at times I would pray and feel almost half dead when I would finish. I remember going in the sanctuary and crying out to God to send in 'reinforcements'. He sure did, He began to sift and to cleanse the temple. There were all kinds of spiritual warfare going on. I witnessed the manipulation of those who wanted control. I felt the spirit of intimidation at times. I needed back up. Who could I trust?

Then the big bang came: the older saint whom so many looked up to decided that she was leaving. She functioned at the time as one of our board members and

was well respected. As soon as she made the announcement that she was leaving, other families started to
leave. Even parts of the roof of the building started
caving in on my husband's office and in the Sunday
school rooms. The building was deemed unsafe, but not
only that, the whole foundation was being shaken. It
was devastating. Not now, when we should be pulling
together. Why are you going too? I wanted to ask. But, I
must be brave, for my husband's sake. I won't let them
see me sweat. No one really gave a good reason; they
just up and left.

A storm with the intensity and force of the Euroclydon,
which the apostle Paul faced in his day, came in and
just about did us in. Henry's grandmother passed away
and he had to go to Jamaica for her funeral. I was not
well, neither physically or emotionally and now my husband was leaving. My son and I experienced one of the
darkest moments of our lives during this season. It was
as though the forces of evil came out in droves to divide
and conquer. But God! God stepped in and strengthened me to weather the storm.

When the cloud lifted a bit, my husband conferred
with the Presbyter of the district and he advised us to
give up the building. With most of the tithe payers gone,
it was quite difficult to continue the upkeep of this
building. But the eternal God is our refuge; He was and
still is in control. When it seemed all hope was gone,
He stepped in, just in the nick of time. We had decided
to give up the building since the owner was not willing
to repair it. He had retired and moved to Florida. We
decided to have church at home. We thought that we
would have fifty percent participation. But no, one lady
told my husband that she could not come to church in
our home; she needed a church building.

Discouragement and failure came in side by side to
visit us the first Sunday after the 'shut-down'. I thought
my breath was going to stop at any moment. How could

they, after all we had done together. But, it was obvious we were not 'together'. We still owed the last month's rent and did not know where it would come from.

The next Sunday morning, we received a whole lot of encouragement. I remember getting ready for worship at home; my husband had gone out to the mailbox. We forgot to check for mail the day before. Then he came in with tears in his eyes and handed me an envelope with nine $100 dollar bills. We had not told anyone about the month's rent that we owed on the building. Somehow God had laid it on someone's heart and they sent a little note to say, "Pastor Brash, thank you for all your hard work in our town". To this day, we do not know who sent the note or the money.......an angel perhaps?

Whenever we think about that we rejoice in knowing that the Lord will help us right to the end. He will not let us be ashamed. It just seems like He waits until the last minute. I guess, to see if we really trust Him. He's like that!

So, as time went on we kept having church in our home or at school buildings. In 1997, we met another couple who were pastors in Milwaukee. They felt led by the Lord to support the ministry for four years. During this transition the financial support was well received and utilized. They planted a seed and now they are, with the help of the Lord, expanding their territory.

The Return of Tolosa-Hunt

April 1998 came in with a bang. We were now in a very nice house, which we hoped to purchase through a land contract. We entered into the arrangement primarily because of the convenience of having church in the basement. It could potentially seat 35. We were so excited and so was the one Sister who stayed with us from the previous group.

We started to see some growth. Families from the area started to respond to our invitations. The excitement grew. Then one day I went in to work and 'it' started again. I noticed the symptoms at different intervals. For weeks I would get these figures dancing before my eyes. Sometimes, I would experience a 'white-out' and I would immediately try to relax until that fearful moment would pass.

So on this particular day in August, I went to work as usual but I became quite ill. My co-workers called the paramedics and had me rushed to the Lake Forest Hospital. They upped my potassium and tried to figure out what else was going on in my body. But that was all they detected. As the days progressed, I realized that I could not see out of both my eyes at times. I would be driving and all of a sudden the vehicles in front of me would just simply disappear. That was quite scary. So I went back to the Neurologist who had treated me previously. He sent me to do another MRI and it showed more or less the same affliction was trying to rise up again. So, once again, I was put on Prednisone. They prescribed a lower dose this time.

I was so frustrated with the whole thing. One Wednesday morning I tried to make contact with the National Organization for rare disorders. As I waited for someone to answer, my other line beeped. I clicked over and heard an African accent on the other end.

He said, "Sister Pauline, the Lord told me to call and pray for you. I don't know what's going on but I want you to put your hand on the spot and believe while I pray." I did as he said and the power and anointing of God visited me in the house. I began to shout, speak in tongues and magnifying God. Just the very thought that I was receiving a call from South Africa was enough for me. That God was so mindful of me was enough to kick my faith sky high. Oh glory!

It felt like a heavy blanket had just been lifted off me and had flown out the door, never to return again. What was also awesome about this was that we had only met once, in 1995. My husband and I graduated at the same time with him from The International College of Grace and Truth and they had exchanged church business cards at that time. We never had any further communication with him. Apparently, he felt a prompting in his spirit, a few days before he made the call, and had to pray and ask the Lord to show him where the number was. After he found the book, he still had to go through the operator to get the correct number since we had moved from Waukegan to Zion. What a God!

After he hung up, I called my husband at work and told him what had just taken place. He just started to sob out of gratitude and amazement at what God had done. We were humbled to think that the Lord was so mindful of us. I told him that I was going to the Workout Center. I was tired of looking like 'pudgy'.

In 1999, Pastor Stephen Zondo visited a church in Chicago and we both testified about this incident in the service that night. He stated something that he had not told me in our first telephone conversation. If he had not prayed for me when he did, I was going to die. I'm not afraid of dying, but what happened a few nights before he called, made me think about what he said.

I was so sick that I could not go upstairs to my bedroom. So Andrew and Claudene decided to come over and stay for a week so she could stay with me in the daytime while Henry went to work. On this particular night, I had a vision in which our house was under siege. I could see the helicopter hovering over the house and the searchlight was on. I knew they were not friendly and proceeded to call out. In the vision it was as if I knew that my husband and Andrew were upstairs. Claudene was on the other couch beside me. They obviously could not hear me and the next thing I knew it was like a window had appeared by the north wall of the family room. Immediately I saw a very intimidating man looking directly at me but saying nothing. He couldn't come into the room but stood outside with the most hateful look on his face.

He looked like a General in the Army, but I knew that he was not good and friendly. I picked up a pen and stabbed him in the face and he fell back and just simply disappeared. A doorway appeared and I walked outside to see where he had fallen. I saw a brass nameplate on the ground but couldn't make out a name. I believe I would have seen a name if it were important.

These experiences have taught me that we are constantly in spiritual warfare. The devil tries to intimidate us by putting fear into our hearts. We must be vigilant and stay focused on the purpose for which the Lord has called us. He will try to distract us by using any means necessary. We must keep our eyes on the prize of the high calling of God in Christ Jesus our Lord.

I was completely delivered from that sickness. The only residual evidence that I was ever afflicted is my inability to hold a pen or pencil to write as I used to.

A new phase

One Sunday morning, after heavy rains, we found about three inches of water on the basement floor. Everything that was on the ground was soaked, even the CPU for the computer. We lost some files but were able to retrieve most. Praise the Lord who promised in Isaiah 43 that the floods shall not overflow us.

The house we were in was in foreclosure and the men with whom we were doing business turned out to be dishonest. They should not have even entered into a sale agreement with us. So we went in search of another building to house the church and found one right in the heart of Zion. We had a wonderful kick-off service in which there were well over 70 in attendance. People were sitting on the floors it was so packed. Two other Pastors had come to support us and had brought their congregation with them. What a time we had.

Then, approximately one year after we were in the building a pipe broke underground and water began to flow in the back of the building where the restroom was located. Can you just see us trying to be discreet so our visitors that morning would not be alarmed? We eventually had to alert them since the bathroom could not be used. That was a hard test, since there were children in the congregation. One lady literally had to take her grandsons to the bathroom at McDonalds up the street. I was happy to see them come back for the end of the service. The Lord had really blessed us with some faithful saints and we prayed that they would be encouraged to stay and see things through.

We attempted to purchase a building of our own, but were turned down by the City. We felt that the Lord still had a better plan. He said He knows the plans He has for us, to give us a hope and a future and an expected end. He also is well able to complete what He has begun. The doors were opened for us to use another church building for our worship services on Sundays. We met in homes for weekly Bible Studies and even taught Bible studies on the job. The Lord showed up every time we met as we hungered for Him.

Our worship services are phenomenal regardless of the number of people who attend. We are learning to feed the Lord with true worship and He just keeps on pouring out the blessings.

I know He has great plans for this work in Zion and a tremendous revival has begun...my prayer is that we will be right in the middle of it when it breaks out and by God's help, we will!

So when your challenges come and you feel like you cannot go another step, just remember "Your dreams should be greater than your memories", and "what's to come, is better than what's been!"

Chapter 10

IN RETROSPECT – MOVING FORWARD

...hitherto hath the LORD helped us-I Sam 7:12

In Retrospect

Looking back in retrospect over all the challenges and changes that we have gone through, we are convinced that we are in the perfect will of God. While we were going through some things, we felt like we were failing the test miserably, but now I see that He was with us all the way. I think of King David when he was surrounded by so many enemies. He even had an anointed enemy in the person of King Saul. They both anointed, yet Saul's worship went sour while David's worship to his God just soared and was perfected.

David wanted Zion. But there were some unwelcome inhabitants, the Jebusites. They told him and his men, 'you'll never come in here'. Mockingly they said, 'even the blind and the lame can keep you out!'. That just further strengthened David's desire for the city. So he and his men went in to fight.

However, this was a test to see who was on the Lord's side. He told his men, there is only one way to conquer the Jebusites and that is through the water shaft or gutter. Anyone who was willing to go through the gutter would become a chief or captain. So, David and his men conquered the Jebusites. They built up Zion and made it a fortress and headquarters.

I am encouraged to think that God would have chosen Henry and myself to come to this 'Zion' for such a time as this. We have come through some things which have helped to fortify our confidence in our God. We could have 'camped' out at each point of failure, but something inside so strong kept telling us to go on.

From time to time some well wishing friends of ours would come and encourage us to give up Zion. They have told us that our ministry would be more effective if we just evangelized. Still we have held on, because we know assuredly that, 'He who has begun the good work in us is able to perform it until the day of Jesus Christ!' (See Phil 1:6).

One of the joys of ministry is also to go out with my husband to encourage other men and women of God. We celebrate a dual ministry and we are honored that God has chosen to use our singing and preaching to bless people everywhere we go. We have ministered all over the United States, Canada and Jamaica. We rely on the anointing to show up in every service and destroy the yoke!

It was on one of our visits to Decatur, Illinois that the Lord spoke to me very clearly about His interest in what we were doing. We were at a point in our ministry where we could just give it all up and move on. The Pastor invited us to come and minister in his Sunday service. After ministering in song, I had just gone back to my seat and settled down to hear the Word of God preached by my husband. I opened my Bible and Hebrews 6:10 just sort of jumped out at me, 'For God is not unrighteous to forget your work and labor of love, which ye have shown toward His Name, in that ye have ministered to the saints and do minister.'

I cannot begin to tell you just how encouraged we were. You see, so many stigmas had been attached to us even by well meaning folks who are so unwise in their conversation with us and others. There were those who made us feel at times that God could not have really called us to Zion and allowed us to go through the stuff that we had gone through.

Reading about David and his men and how they conquered Zion is a real encouragement. Let me encourage you right now in your circumstances. You may be faced with the challenge of your lifetime. Others are telling you what they deem the will of God is for your life. You need to know for yourself!

God is well able to bring you into your fullest potential. He promises never to leave you nor forsake you. There, I said it again! If you believe that He has called you for a particular ministry, when you feel the rays of doubt plaguing your soul, go back to God. He will make it plain for you.

Henry and I had to overcome so many obstacles and are still overcoming. We are in the 28th year of our marriage, with three married children who have given us ten grandchildren. We endeavor to maintain a good relationship with our family. The church is ultimately, God's. It is His family and He will not let it die. He has to present it to Himself, holy, blameless and without spot or wrinkle.

We have had to forge through some ugly stuff to keep that godly relationship with our God and family. We refuse to accept anyone stigmatizing us. A stigma is a stain or reproach on one's character. There are people in this world whom we have encountered on our journey, whose calling in life is seemingly to make other people's lives miserable.

We are passionate about breaking the negative cycles that have existed for generations. I love it when my daughter Charmaine reiterates, 'Mums, we are cycle breakers'. I have learned so much from her and Jonathan, her husband. I have watched their sacrifice to reach the ultimate in God.

Every day of my life I plead the blood of Jesus over my husband and I. I pray over our relationship with God, our children, grandchildren, extended family, church family, and so on. It is only by the blood of Jesus that we are cleansed of every stigma, curse, wounds, criticisms and anything else that's potentially damaging to you. The Apostle Paul encourages us to forget the things that are behind and move forward to the prize of the high calling of God in Christ Jesus

When I think about stigma, I think about a young man by the name of Jabez. His mother named him Jabez because she said in I Chronicles 4:9, '... I gave birth to him with pain'. He cried out to the God of Israel, 'Oh that you would bless me and enlarge my territory! Let your hand be with me, and keep me from harm so that I will be free from pain.' And God granted his request.

We can turn our situation around by beginning to focus on Jesus. Jabez did not focus on the stigma that his mother placed on him. He cursed the curse. He triumphed and I know by the help of the Lord, we will also.

We are learning so much side by side. We are learning to not be anxious for anything. 'They that wait upon the Lord shall renew their strength; they shall mount up with wings as eagles, they shall run and not be weary, and they shall walk and not faint.' Isaiah: 40:28.

We have only just begun. We are in the prime of our lives and are very excited about the exploits that the Lord will enable us to perform. I believe that He has given us the City, so...

Until then our hearts will go on singing
Until then with joy we'll carry on
Until the day our eyes behold the city
Until the day, God calls us home!

Be encouraged man of God, woman of God. Do not listen to the lies of the devil. Keep your focus on Christ. You, who are pregnant with the WORD and desire to give birth, cry out unto your God. Ask Him to enlarge your territory. There are so many souls yet to be born in the Kingdom.

You are precious to Him. You are the apple of His eyes. He will not forget your labor of love. Stay on the firing line. Do not quit, better is on before.

Husbands and wives in ministry, whatever you do, do not blame each other for the negativities on your journey. It is not your fault. Do not blame yourself for the failures of others. Pace yourselves. Spend time away together to renew your relationship with each other. You are responsible and accountable for your relationship with each other.

Remember, healthy families, healthy churches. Work on your relationships at home. The church is the business of the King.

I am blessed to be a part of an awesome healing and deliverance ministry with my devoted husband and friend Henry. We presently serve as Worship Chaplains and Pastors of The New Horizons International Ministries operating out of the Midwestern Regional Medical/Cancer Center in Zion, Illinois.

In 2004, God's favor was once again poured out upon me. That year, my solo project "Transition" was sponsored by a wonderful Pastor in North Miami. It is still being a tool of praise and worship to our God and many are encouraged when they listen to my songs.

I am also a Quality Assurance Auditor at one of the most thriving and successful pharmaceutical companies here in the Midwest which has afforded us the privilege of acquiring a comfortable lifestyle.

"Now unto Him that is able to keep you from falling, and to present you faultless before the presence of His glory with exceeding joy; to the only wise God our Savior, be glory and majesty, dominion and power, both now and ever. Amen"

MOVING FORWARD!

I Confess and Declare Today

I am steadfast and immovable! I have a non-negotiable attitude of absolute determination to do what God has called me to do. I am fixed, solid, grounded, established, anchored, unvarying, permanent, and stable in my tenacity to grab hold of all that God has destined for me to accomplish with my life. I will not stop, give in, give up, or surrender to anything that tries to discourage me or to throw me off track. I am committed to stay in the race until I've made it all the way to the end. I declare this by faith in Jesus' name!

1 Corinthians 15:58
Therefore, my beloved brethren, be ye steadfast, un-moveable, always abounding in the work of the Lord...

The true Zion awaits!

THANK YOU,

To My Family: Henry, Andrew, Charmaine and Michelle, thank you for holding on down through the years. You have helped to shape and develop me into who I am today.

To the Editors: Lois Morris, Judy Kannenberg, Pranob Bhattacharya, Michelle Antoinette and my husband of 28 years, Henry Abraham – You have all done a phenomenal job, and now look at the priceless treasure that we have!

To Pastor W.S. Stewart: Thank you for touching my life again with such words of affirmation as presented in the Foreword.

CPSIA information can be obtained at www.ICGtesting.com
Printed in the USA
243159LV00002B/2/P